American Covenant

AMERICAN
COVENANT

NATIONAL PARKS,
THEIR PROMISE, AND
OUR NATION'S FUTURE

MICHAEL A. SOUKUP

GARY E. MACHLIS

Yale
UNIVERSITY PRESS

New Haven and London

Published with assistance from the foundation established in memory of Amasa Stone Mather of the Class of 1907, Yale College.

Yale University Press books may be purchased in quantity for educational, business, or promotional use. For information, please email sales. press@yale.edu (US office) or sales@yaleup.co.uk (UK office).

Set in Gotham and Adobe Garamond types by IDS Infotech Ltd.
Printed in the United States of America.

ISBN 978-0-300-14035-4 (alk. paper)
Library of Congress Control Number: 2020943782
A catalogue record for this book is available from the British Library.

This paper meets the requirements of ANSI/NISO Z39.48-1992
(Permanence of Paper).

10 9 8 7 6 5 4 3 2 1

To our children and grandchildren

Contents

American Covenant

Mount Rainier National Park.
Iconic national parks like Mount Rainier inspire Americans.
(Photograph by Sage Ross)

1

Good Fortune

There is a vast, strange, and beautiful place at the southern tip of Florida that every American should see. The Everglades, with its expanse of water fifty miles wide in places, has for thousands of years flowed slowly over porous limestone, sand, and peat from Lake Okeechobee to the Gulf of Mexico. In the poetic phrase of Marjory Stoneman Douglas, this "river of grass" is quietly majestic, fecund, and richly alive.[1] It is a subtropical paradise or a foreboding wilderness, depending on how you approach it. Experiences in the Everglades are often unforgettable.

The Everglades system receives water from as far north as Orlando via overflows from Lake Okeechobee. Its flat terrain and shallow waters dominate South Florida. Along the way, the "glades" are made up of sawgrass prairies, tree islands, hardwood hammocks (where slight elevations allow their growth), marl prairies, cypress stands, freshwater sloughs, pinelands, coastal prairies, mangrove swamps, and the marine and brackish areas along Florida Bay. Guidebooks list its marvelous wildlife in our national vernacular: American alligators and American crocodiles; Florida redbelly, soft-shell, and loggerhead turtles; green tree and leopard frogs; apple snails; Florida panthers and bobcats; zebra butterflies; swallowtail kites, Everglades snail kites, limpkins, roseate spoonbills, brown pelicans, and anhingas; great blue, white, and green herons; wood storks, snowy egrets, white ibises, purple gallinules, white-crowned pigeons, barred owls, black vultures, flamingos, and bald eagles. The wide range of curious things to see goes on: manatees, mangrove snappers, largemouth bass, oscars, mosquitofish, Florida gars, crayfish, blue crabs, coon oysters, pink shrimp, and tarpons; spatterdocks, black and red mangroves, native orchids, and so many more.[2] Some twenty-three species of native snakes, including six poisonous ones, add to the Everglades' image as a stark, somewhat foreboding, but compelling place. Here wildlife stalks, slithers, and swims among millions of acres of sawgrass, swamp lilies, bull thistles, strap ferns, air plants, gumbo limbo trees, slash pines, royal palms, saw-palmettos, strangler figs, and dwarf cypress. The Everglades' authenticity as a desolate and starkly beautiful destination attracts adventurers from all over the world.

The Everglades has been in many ways America's last eastern frontier. It has held a unique place in America's human history, replete with pirates, politicians, plume hunters, alligator poachers, and assorted outlaws. Long before that it was home to Native Americans such as the Calusa and the Miami, and it remains to this day the home of the Cow Creek Seminole and the Miccosukee peoples. More recently the Everglades has also stood in the way of South Florida's rapacious appetite for development.

While stubbornly resisting huge public and private projects to drain it entirely, by the early twentieth century the Everglades was being diminished to the extent that there was mounting concern that this one-of-a-kind place needed protection or it would be forever lost. A large portion of the glades just below Lake Okeechobee had already become the Everglades Agricultural Area—700,000 acres of sugar cane fields and vegetable farms—as huge public works projects were beginning to control floods and provide for agricultural and municipal water supplies. Massive public works projects enabled constant human encroachment along its periphery, with cities, suburbs, universities, and farms occupying areas that were once Everglades wetlands.

Eventually responding to public concern for the Everglades as a unique and biologically important wetland, Congress authorized a national park for the Everglades in 1935. There followed a great struggle among competing interests that both delayed the park's formal establishment and limited its extent. Finally, in 1947 a significant segment of the southern Everglades was set aside by President Harry Truman with great ceremony as a national park, to be protected for generations to come. This was a scaled-down version of the conservationists' ideal, but it was the compromise necessary to move the idea forward. Big Cypress National Preserve and Biscayne National Park were later designated to include protection of some of the original features of Everglades protection that the conservation-minded had proposed.[3]

Everglades National Park was something new, a national park established to protect the southern Everglades, its strange wildness, and its curious intersection of temperate and tropical plants and animals. It was to be a national park without majestic mountains; indeed, the park has a maximum elevation of 10 feet over its 1.5 million acres. There is no breathtaking canyon or giant trees. It was the first park established largely to protect the biology of an immense and complicated wetland. The struggle to preserve this precious place is an object lesson for the broader struggles facing the preservation of national parks across America. A key objective in establishing the national park at the downstream end of the Everglades was to preserve the colonies of wading birds—ibises, wood storks, and egrets—whose massive flights once could block out the sun, as well as a significant portion of the Everglades' subtropical assemblage of alligators, crocodiles, snail kites, Florida panthers, and manatees. Today there remain places in the park where you can trek or boat and see a half dozen endangered species in an afternoon.

Yet by the 1960s the wading bird colonies were declining, and by the 1970s and 1980s, most were gone. The most widely cited (though somewhat poorly documented) estimate suggested that there had been a 90 percent decline.[4] It was becoming clear that providing national park status, in and of itself, had not guaranteed protection of the Everglades from the consequences of intense development outside its boundary. South Florida's demand for flood control, crop irrigation, and water supply was disrupting the processes that created and maintained the Everglades ecosystem.

Ominously, a mere decade after park designation, the managers of Everglades National Park found themselves failing in their mission. Worse, they had no clear understanding of why the decline in nesting wading birds was happening or what should be done to reverse the demise of one of the park's signature resources. The traditions and within-boundary management successes of the great western parks had little relevance to a park that was dependent on a landscape rapidly changing thanks to human hubris and interference.

Although the Everglades story is an extreme example of a park in peril, many other parks today are surrounded by changing landscapes and processes beyond their managers' understanding and control. The fundamental lesson from the Everglades is that, if national parks are to persist, national park staffs must, first and foremost, have an in-depth science-based understanding of the resources they manage and an effective means of sharing that understanding with advocates and decision makers at all levels of our society. Herein we seek to champion a solid science foundation for park management as an absolute requirement for the salvation of America's grand National Park System and its reflection of our extraordinary natural heritage.

We also hope to convey the urgency of the need to begin the process of incorporating science into the daily business of every national park. As this will require major institutional and cultural change in the agency that manages national parks, there is no time to waste. In later chapters we offer our thoughts on what needs to be done to truly protect national parks.

Places that remain familiar to each of us over time anchor both our personal stories and our sense of identity. In like manner, creating national parks anchors us as a nation by keeping places intact that have shaped our history and identity. This requires an unbroken commitment in each generation and across succeeding generations. We write to convey an understanding of the elements of the covenant between generations of Americans that is necessary to ensure consistent protection of national parks over time. Drawing attention to the nature and necessity of this distinctive American covenant is perhaps our most essential reason for writing this book.

As with the nation as a whole, national park experiences influence us as individuals in many positive ways. One piece of evidence for this is reflected in the voluble community to be found around the world of those who are fascinated by and grateful for their connection to national parks. Many are visitors, and if you have opened this book, chances are you share the good fortune of having visited one or more of America's national parks. Others are academics who spend their careers studying the science, law, or history of parks. A few of you may have had the opportunity to work in, near, or for national parks—as rangers, scientists, resource managers, maintenance workers, seasonal park staff, concession employees, even bureaucrats in the government agency that manages these special places—the National Park Service. We, Mike and Gary, are scientists whose experience represents more than seventy-five years in those various categories of experience with national parks.

This book stems from our decades-long series of visits to America's national parks and the truths we have discovered about their value and their vulnerability. We believe both their value and their vulnerability are broadly underestimated and that a full understanding of these aspects will lead to urgent action by every American. This, too, is why we write.

Public service results in many forms of personal education, and we have learned valuable (and sometimes difficult) lessons in the service of national parks. Our good fortune in our careers in the National Park Service (NPS) extends to the wide range of experiences and adventures we have had along the way and what the parks and those who care about them have taught us. These lessons compel us to describe why parks matter—in fact, why they are *vital*—to our nation's future.

We offer our personal experiences and our thoughts on how the preservation and enjoyment of the national parks can be advanced in the twenty-first century. We focus on national parks that preserve and protect nature; the extraordinary collection of historic and cultural parks deserve their own and special treatment.

Our method is to share a series of short narratives that illustrate and express our point of view. We hope this book of reflections by veteran park scientists can add useful perspective to the growing collection of park-related texts, essays, travelogues, and polemics available to the reader. As for many people, our strong connection to national parks is deeply personal.

So how did two scientists, one trained in sociology and the other in limnology (freshwater ecology), find themselves in Washington, D.C., engaged in the leadership and management of the national parks through three administrations? We begin with our individual stories and how we came to our long visit with national parks.

Gary grew up in the Pacific Northwest under the shoulders of Mount Rainier. The mountain and the national park surrounding it were to play important roles in his youth, as was typical of many young persons in the region. His grandparents emigrated from Eastern Europe via Ellis Island to Philadelphia and then west to Seattle. Later his parents made a shorter, still common, journey from a modest old house in Seattle's urban center to a modest new house on Mercer Island—a suburbanizing island in Lake Washington, outside the city but inside its economic and cultural orbit. His family moved into a new tract development typical of the early 1960s. The Douglas fir forest had been cleared ("slicked" is the technical term) for a new crop of suburban split-level homes. The houses rose out of earth cleared of all vegetation, arranged along artificial streets that led only to other, similar, houses.

The remnant of forest behind the house (named "the Woods" by local convention) emphasized what had been taken and how little remained, with the additional benefit of being full of adventure and surprise for children (no adults would bother visiting, much to the kids' delight). Hours of discovery were spent in the Woods. Toys, lunches, jackets, and shirts were left behind; stones, leaves, small mammal bones, and other treasures were brought home.

Like many suburban pioneers, Gary's parents built patios and fences, planted lawns and flowerbeds, and reforested the land with an exotic and nonsensical mix of trees—river birch on the upland slope, Japanese maple next to driveways, juniper along the flowerbeds, and no Douglas fir. His father painted the siding, finished off the basement with asbestos ceiling tiles and dark plywood paneling, and commuted each day into the city, with the weekends spent in a cycle of fertilizing to make the grass grow tall and mowing to keep the grass cut short.

All the while, Mount Rainier loomed in the near distance. On clear days, the mountain dominates the regional skyline and orients the geography for northwesterners. On the many cloudy days, it is out of sight but not out of mind. In the 1960s Rainier was still a technical climb for the experienced mountaineer, and one of Gary's heroes, Jim Whittaker, famously trained for Everest on the mountain. A family trip to Mount Rainier's ice caves (now disappeared as the glaciers have receded) was unforgettable; years later Gary can picture the picnic table under the curved ice roof, sandwiches eaten in the chill of the cave, and the vibrant blue light—an extraordinary blue—filtering through the ice cave's opening.

Typical of many young boys in the region, he became a Boy Scout. Joining Boy Scouts was less about uniforms and badges of merit and more about manipulating an adult into driving Gary and his friends to Mount Rainier to hike and explore. The equipment—Trapper Nelson backpacks that made even light loads heavy, cotton sleeping bags that turned into fearsome weights when wet, and #10 tin cans for cooking—were no impediment to enthusiasm for the mountain. Hiking and camping were primary childhood pleasures, and Mount Rainier sat silently, challenging Gary to do more.

When he came of age to drive the family station wagon, Boy Scouts was abandoned, trips to Rainier were with teenage friends, and high school led to college. He settled on studying forestry at the University of Washington in Seattle under the shoulders of the mountain. His ineptitude with plant identification and empathy for persons, families, and communities shifted his studies toward the social sciences. At the time, the National Park Service was beginning to realize it needed an understanding of park visitors, and working for Don Field (one of the first social scientists in the NPS), Gary began graduate work. His first project involved developing environmental education materials for Mount Rainier National Park. Finishing forestry training, teaching at a nearby college, and pondering what path to follow, he began to read widely. Sometime along the way, he climbed and summitted Mount Rainier with his younger brother in a group organized by Whittaker's climbing business.

One of the books he read was *Daydreams and Nightmares: A Sociological Essay on the American Environment,* by William R. Burch, Jr.[5] It electrified him, suggesting that interests in environmental and social issues could be fruitfully combined. Burch was teaching at Yale, so Gary traveled there to study with Burch and complete his Ph.D. As he had never been east of Bozeman, Montana, life at Yale and in the eastern United States was as different as interplanetary travel, or so it seemed at the time. While at New Haven, Gary would drive each Friday several hours north to Keene, New Hampshire, to teach part-time at Antioch Graduate School. A northwesterner comfortable with the constant green of Douglas fir forests mixed occasionally with ponderosa pine, and even more rarely madrona trees and rhododendron, Gary was stunned by the fall colors of New England, which more than once compelled him to pull off the New Hampshire roads and stare in wide-eyed wonder. Finishing at Yale, he (with a young family in tow) quickly returned to the Pacific Northwest, educated and impoverished.

At the time, the National Park Service was setting up research units at several universities in the region, including the University of Idaho, where Gary interviewed with the dean of the forestry college, John Ehrenreich. Ehrenreich was unsure about adding a social scientist to his faculty but had a vision of the college as a leader in all forms of science useful to natural resources management. They discussed the university, the location, the weather, and mutual acquaintances. Ehrenreich then gently asked, "If I gave you a job, what would you do? Could you come back tomorrow with a plan?"

That night, Gary outlined a plan of research and teaching that was to center on national parks in the United States and around the world, and was to last for over three decades.

Mike—though he rose to the highest ranks of the National Park Service leadership—had no early definitive national park experience like Gary's with Mount Rainier. His father was one of seven children of Czech immigrants who somehow found their way to Richmond, Virginia; most Czechs went to farm in the Midwest. Mike's mother was the only child of an old southern family from Albemarle County. Located halfway between Fair Oaks and Seven Pines, their few acres of land supported goats, chickens, rabbits, and a garden of corn, watermelons, and beans. His 1950s rural childhood was blessed with a summer cabin on Windmill Point, where the Rappahannock River joins the Chesapeake Bay. The modest hunting cabin was on an undeveloped shoreline where Mike would walk sandy beaches for miles at dawn, encountering little but nature and the occasional arrowhead washed from the eroding shoreline. Large heron colonies nesting in the pines would send up hundreds of wheeling, croaking Great Blues each time he passed along the beach. In summers he was tormented by stinging nettles in the rivers and mosquitoes on land, and his early career fantasies focused on learning enough biology to destroy them all.

At that time in rural Virginia, birds of prey had a bounty of fifty cents on their heads—they were thought to take prey that people had the sole right to; crows were also fair game, but more than a match for his hunting skills. He saw life in terms of pitting oneself against nature. His career as a hunter ended the moment it was first successful, planting a seed of wildlife protection that would gradually replace his early hunter-gatherer mindset. When a series of hurricanes in the late 1950s took his family's waterfront and cabin, outdoor activities once again became limited to reaping the spring shad run, frog gigging, foraging for mushrooms, and fishing the Chickahominy and Piankatank Rivers.

A family car-camping trip to Key West when Mike was six took him through Everglades National Park along the Tamiami Trail to Naples, Florida. He remembers the alligators and the Miccosukee Indian village, and also seeing the roadhouse along the trail that somehow had a twin-engine plane perched on its roof as if taking off. Only later in his National Park Service career did he learn that the roadhouse had been a brothel in the 1950s; it eventually became a visitor center for Big Cypress National Preserve—a minor triumph in adaptive reuse of buildings with an interesting history. Although at the time he had little comprehension that he was in a national park, when Mike arrived as director of research for Everglades National Park in 1989, memories of the landscape returned and may have cushioned his transition from the Boston suburbs. A recurring tenet of this book will be the value of opportunities to revisit places over decades and rediscover them intact.

At the University of Richmond, Mike was drawn to field ecology. In the 1960s developmental biology and physiology were considered serious biological pursuits; marine biology and ecology were not. Yet Mike was fascinated by the idea of "food from the sea," a popular concept at the time extolling the capability of oceans to feed everyone indefinitely. He soon learned enough ecology to reconsider his dream of eradicating all the nettlesome species of his childhood.

After graduation his adviser, John Bishop, called to tell him of a technician job opening at the Marine Biological Laboratory in Woods Hole, Massachusetts. Mike was soon making his first sojourn out of the South. The laboratory promptly sent him on his first trip to New York City for an oceanography conference, where he happened on an elevator full of Russian and American scientists (a rare event in the late 1960s). They were arguing about the wisdom of extrapolating high coastal photosynthesis rates across the great expanse of mostly barren open oceans. This practice had apparently led the Soviets and others to overestimate the harvestable bounty of the oceans. Soon thereafter, the Russians ceased investing in huge factory ships designed to harvest levels of fish populations that the oceans were never capable of sustaining. The panacea of inexhaustible food from the sea was an illusion. Mike had to find another cause.

Aside from the general cultural shock of New England, the community of Woods Hole exposed him to many new things, including a new appreciation for recreation in protected areas. Group camping in October snow on the Appalachian Trail in the White Mountains of

New Hampshire was entirely new. The Appalachian Trail with its system of huts open to all was eye-opening.

With year-round experience as a deckhand and scuba diver, Mike was captured by the oceanographer's world but physically chilled enough from February dives off Nantucket to consider graduate school as a better alternative. He was accepted to the new oceanography program being created at the University of Massachusetts, Amherst, and arrived in the fall of 1968. It was a tumultuous time of protest and alternative lifestyles. Reports of a semester of campus anarchy, including many evenings of bonfires and long lines of nude anarchist youths dancing in the firelight, so frightened Massachusetts legislators that they abandoned plans to further enlarge the student body, and they drastically cut the university's budget. Instantly new departments such as oceanography were gone. Ever adaptive, Mike switched to limnology, the study of inland lakes, rivers, ponds, and wetlands. "Upland oceanography" was a more practical lifestyle anyway for an impoverished graduate student with two children. He studied the biogeochemistry of silica in mountain lakes and watersheds in the Berkshires.

The exciting opportunity to apply science amid the complexities of the real world came one day as he was finishing his dissertation. The phone rang in his major professor's laboratory. Usually this meant a consulting job. If the professor was not there, his graduate students scrambled to get to the phone. With two kids and a below-poverty-level stipend, Mike often won the footrace.

This call was from Larry Hadley, the superintendent of Cape Cod National Seashore—a new unit of the National Park System. He needed advice. Members of the local press were reporting that some local freshwater lakes—popular swimming holes that were part of the national seashore—were in fact public health nuisances. An industrious undergraduate summer volunteer had found some serious pathogens in Wellfleet's kettle ponds (remnants of the receding glaciers) that were heavily used by park visitors, some of whom were reporting ear infections. Armed with a bacteriological testing kit but without performing any confirmatory tests, the student was posting on the town bulletin board his discoveries of pathogens never found before in freshwater lakes. The local papers were charging the superintendent with endangering public health.

Mike asked Superintendent Hadley about the ponds—were they shallow or deep? "Don't know," he said. Saltwater or fresh? Groundwater fed? "The park has no idea," said the superintendent. Mike asked how one managed a national park without knowing anything about the resources. Hadley laughed and said to come on down to the Cape and "let's talk about what we need to know."

During the following year of study at Cape Cod National Seashore, Mike filled out each and every government form requested of him—he treated them like amusing crossword puzzles. This apparent respect for bureaucracy was a rare occurrence in the regional office's experience with scientists, and Mike was soon invited to apply for a permanent job with the National Park Service in Boston.

On his first day in the North Atlantic Regional Office, Mike met a beaming chief of the lands acquisition division, who had just purchased the Fountain Avenue Landfill in Brooklyn, New York, to become part of Gateway National Recreation Area. Gateway was a new urban park designed to introduce the National Park System to urban populations. This new parcel of land had formerly been the world's largest truck-filled landfill (and was now "high ground"—the original Mount Trashmore, perhaps) on the edge of Jamaica Bay. It was famous for hosting the "midnight dumpers." These trucking companies, though contracted to transport industrial toxic wastes to approved hazardous waste disposal facilities, found it more profitable to eliminate the expense and bother of traveling to designated hazardous waste disposal sites in New Jersey. Rather, with the facilitation of the city's landfill manager (who was by then serving time for criminal mischief), the trucks would pull into especially bulldozed pits and release their cargo of toxic materials under cover of night. Millions of gallons of toxic wastes had gone into the landfill—out of sight, out of mind, but free to roam.

"What about the impact of toxic leachates on Jamaica Bay?" Mike asked the lands acquisition chief.

"What's leachate?" answered the chief. Mike instantly knew there was work to do here—perhaps even a cause.

True, the city's well-paid consultants had not yet found any pollutants leaking from the site, thus conveniently expediting the transfer of the city's lands to the federal government. Yet in nature everything leaks, and it wasn't long before massive PCB slicks were discovered (no consulting fees required) by local fishermen casting their lines where the unconfined landfill met the tidal waters of Jamaica Bay.

Mike knew he had found a suitable 1960s calling. He could contribute something valuable to society and for a cause one could truly believe in—providing the science necessary to maintain nature unimpaired (and in many cases begin to restore it) in the small, naive agency responsible for national parks.

Mike's career continued to pivot around phone calls. After the calls leading him to Woods Hole and Cape Cod National Seashore, a call from the superintendent of Everglades National Park encouraged him to apply to be director of the park's South Florida Research Center. And six years later, calls from Washington, D.C., encouraged him to apply for NPS's chief scientist position—officially the associate director, Natural Resource Stewardship and Science. After his stint in the Everglades (described early on as a God-forsaken swamp "suitable only for the haunt of noxious vermin, or the resort of pestilential reptiles") he felt he was ready for Washington, D.C.[6] Once there, Mike found himself in a policy-level position where he could fix some of the problems he had seen as park researcher, regional office scientist, and park division chief.

After he retired in 2007, Mike and his family built a home on Virginia's Great Wicomico River, seventeen miles as the crow flies from the old cabin site on Windmill Point. One day while rocking on the porch, a call led him to direct the Schoodic Education and Research Center at Acadia National Park, and life in Maine.

Occasionally young conservationists ask him how to plan their careers. His answer: "Find a cause, do your best, answer the phone."

Gary went on to have a busy career as a university professor, first at the University of Idaho and now at Clemson University. Along the way he worked with Mike as visiting chief social scientist for the National Park Service (the "visiting" in the title reflecting both Gary's and the agency's tentativeness about the idea) and reported to and was mentored by Mike. Gary then served during both terms of the Obama administration as science adviser to the director of the National Park Service, the first scientist ever appointed to such a position with the NPS.

This book is the product of our combined experience and experiences as scientists, National Park Service leaders, and joyful visitors to America's national parks. We believe that the national parks are an essential, distinctive, and ascendant element of the American experience, vital to the quality of our national future. We have also come to understand that much still must be done to preserve our national parks for the generations to follow. We hope to provide local, regional, and national decision makers; politicians, and their political parties; nongovernmental organizations, scientists, and students; and, most importantly, citizens, with a better knowledge of why parks matter. We also wish to provoke their action to keep this remarkable covenant among and between generations strong and unimpaired.

Glacier Bay National Park.
The National Park Service must understand both natural change and
resource vulnerability to human-caused impacts across the vast span of
resources it manages—from glaciers to whales and much more.
(Courtesy of the U.S. National Park Service)

2

Our Sense of National Parks

Our nation's identity, history, and national character are unique and are shaped in part by North America's natural heritage. The rich continent contained a wide diversity of plants, animals, and persons that has affected all who settle on its landscapes, from the ancient Anasazi and Nez Perce to the nineteenth-century immigrant Irish and recent Sudanese refugees. Our natural heritage has helped forge our nation's character, just as it has fueled its extraordinary achievements and its flawed but inexorable pursuit of high moral ground.

National parks are an important reflection of this heritage and more. At a time when we may not be likely in our frantic daily lives to appreciate this heritage or dwell on our relationship with nature, national parks can remind us of universal connections and responsibilities—to the future of our species, to other species, to our nation and our planet. Later we shall describe these connections and responsibilities as *covenants,* across this generation and with those before and after us.

National parks remind us that the human experience reaches far beyond our own kind; they reconnect us with species we no longer regularly meet, had forgotten—or perhaps, in most cases, never knew. National park experiences bond us with the majesty of nature on this small planet—and remind us that we are but one biological species amid millions—all playing out our lives, gifted with the potential of each new day. The night sky reminds us of mysteries that are far beyond the ken of any species. The darkened firmament in a remote park (Crater Lake National Park in Oregon, Joshua Tree National Park in California, or Dry Tortugas National Park in Florida, for example) confronts us with just how insignificant we are and how special our planet is as a haven in the distances of the universe. Individually, our experiences in national parks can teach us that nature provides an environment that outshines any that can be built or shaped for the needs of any one species.

That national parks teach us humility is of great consequence and value. The herds of bison and elk tested daily by the wolf, marine fossils found on the mountain, and a river's slow chiseling of deep canyons all tell us that the earth's drama isn't just about us, no matter how important or in charge we as a species may feel at the moment.

National parks represent singular promises of restraint requiring that we transcend our immediate wants and needs in a manner that allows both present and future generations to be celebrants of these places. Imagine your great-great-grandchildren looking up in wonder from Yellowstone, Crater Lake, Joshua Tree, or Dry Tortugas, enthralled as you once were with the same clear and beautiful night sky!

Even taking the long view, all reliable evidence to date tells us that the earth outstrips any other option for human habitation. That revelation alone should give us cause for gratitude for its creation. It is tempting to posit that our small "blue marble" of a planet really is the Garden of Eden of the Old Testament. Although there are signs that we as a species are falling out of grace, Eden is still all around us, and living in harmony with it may still be within our grasp. We may be closest to such a state today around a campfire in the backcountry of a national park. Perhaps experiences in parks can inspire and even lead us to a sustainable relationship between our daily lives and the health of the planet. If a fraction of the zeal we can muster as a species for materialism, dogma, and war were redirected toward respect for nature, a sustainable planet might be ours to pass forward to future generations. Few things are more important.

Regrettably, our want for comfort and our tendency toward extravagance as a species comes with a price whose true currency no one knows. We do know that it is taking a toll on the survival of other species and their (and ultimately our own) life-support systems. Every day the world population grows, material expectations rise, and economic activity—with spurts and sputters—compounds its reach and impact. Most people would agree (some reluctantly) that the earth's systems have begun to show discernible signs of significant wear and tear, and some (mostly scientists and recently religious leaders) believe we are close to limits that can permanently close our access to a sustainable planet if we exceed them.

In 2000, the historian J. R. McNeill published *Something New Under the Sun: An Environmental History of the Twentieth-Century World.* He notes: "The human race, without intending anything of the sort, has undertaken a gigantic uncontrolled experiment on the earth. In time, I think, this will appear as the most important aspect of twentieth century history."[1] McNeill argues that we have entered an age that violates the Old Testament adage (Eccl. 9:11) "there is nothing new under the sun." He argues that human dominance of global processes and features (familiar examples include climate change and the ozone layer) is fundamentally different from the more localized boom-bust cycles of populations, cultures, and empires seen throughout history.

Scientists have documented five past episodes in earth's history of major environmental catastrophes that have led to massive extinctions of species. Many are making predictions based on convincing field evidence that we have begun a period of a sixth great extinction of species on earth.[2] Estimates vary widely but tend toward a 50 percent loss of plant and animal species in the twenty-first century. The something new here is that one species of animal is the root cause—not asteroids, volcanoes, or geological time-scale trends in climate.

Aside from new inventions such as chlorofluorohydrocarbons, which in the 1970s were found to be depleting the ozone layer around our planet, it is often the scale and intensity of age-old "traditional" activities like agriculture, timber harvesting, burning, manufacturing, waste production, mining, hunting, and fishing—all amplified by new technology and a burgeoning world population—that have brought us to the brink of this new paradigm of something new under the sun. The fate of the planet is in the hands of one rather troublesome species.

All of this is recognized by top scientists around the world, with few serious science-based challenges. The bad news is that it is hard to see humans as a whole changing their reproductive or acquisitive behavior in time. The only way any of this can be good news is if it awakens us in time to a new era of greater human restraint in what we ask from the earth.

This awakening is being raised by religious leaders as well as the scientific community. In an extraordinary encyclical letter titled *On Care for Our Common Home,* the Catholic Church's Pope Francis calls for "a new and universal solidarity":

> I urgently appeal, then, for a new dialogue about how we are shaping the future of our planet. We need a conversation which includes everyone, since the environment challenge we are undergoing, and its human roots, concern and affect us all. The worldwide ecological movement has already made considerable progress and led to the establishment of numerous organizations committed to raising awareness of these challenges. Regrettably, many efforts to seek concrete solutions to the environmental crisis have proved ineffective, not only because of powerful opposition but also because of a more general lack of interest. Obstructionist attitudes, even

on the part of believers, can range from denial of the problem
to indifference, nonchalant resignation or blind confidence
in technical solutions. We require a new and universal solidarity.[3]

The Buddhist monk Thich Nhat Hanh (nominated for the Nobel
Peace Prize by Martin Luther King, Jr.) echoes this call to awaken in
his book *The World We Have:*

> The bells of mindfulness are sounding. All over the
> Earth, we are experiencing floods, droughts, and massive
> wildfires. Sea ice is melting in the Arctic and hurricanes and
> heat waves are killing thousands. The forests are fast disap-
> pearing, the deserts are growing, species are becoming extinct
> every day, and yet we continue to consume, ignore the
> ringing bells.
>
> All of us know that our beautiful green planet is in dan-
> ger. Our way of walking on the Earth has a great influence on
> animals and plants. Yet we act as if our daily lives have noth-
> ing to do with the condition of the world. We are like sleep-
> walkers, not knowing what we are doing or where we are
> heading. Whether we can wake up or not depends on whether
> we can walk mindfully on our Mother Earth. The future of
> all life, including our own, depends on our mindful steps. We
> have to hear the bells of mindfulness that are sounding all
> across our planet. We have to start learning how to live in a
> way that a future will be possible for our children and our
> grandchildren.[4]

When scientist, pope, and Buddhist monk all call on us to awaken
to this "generational responsibility," we as citizens might be wise to

listen. And if their call to awaken rings true, the changed role of humans on this planet adds importance to why national parks matter.

Perhaps a cautious first step of "mindfulness" would be to save a small representative sample of our natural resource capital—natural resource systems with all of their pieces and processes intact—in a strategic reserve of nature. This would seem a wise choice when the stakes are so high.

More than a hundred years ago, America's National Park System was set up to do just that. A significant part of our nation's inheritance is now vested in this system, managed by a tiny government agency— the National Park Service. What are the "System" and "Service," and how did they come to be?[5]

In the nineteenth century, amid a period of massive despoliation of nature and thirst for natural resources, a movement began to save intact some spectacular examples of this nation's natural heritage. Yellowstone National Park (NP) in Idaho, Montana, and Wyoming and Yosemite National Park in California are perhaps the best-known examples of the early desire to preserve scenic lands intact while elsewhere the forests were cleared, bison slaughtered, predators exterminated, rivers dammed, and prairie plowed. By 1916, the number of parks being established required an agency to manage them, and the National Park Service was born. In simple, elegant language Congress directed the National Park Service in its Organic Act (the quaint phrase referring to the legislation creating a government agency but revered by the agency's employees) "to conserve unimpaired the wild life and the scenery of national parks for the enjoyment of present and future generations." It is important to note that "wild life" was chosen by these particular legislators carefully. Some of these legislators were casual naturalists, typical of the privileged in those times—collectors of butterflies, beetles, plants, fossils, and so forth. Their intent was to protect not just game animals (often synonymous with the term "wildlife"), but all the interconnected and dynamic parts that constituted nature's "scenery." Herein we use the term "wild life" as meaning the full range of diverse species living in the wild and "wildlife" as referring to the more familiar species that most people recognize and often associate with hunting.

This history is complicated by the legacy of Native American and rural poor removals from their traditional homelands that were to become national parks. Indigenous peoples lived on, relied on, and stewarded lands now national parks—from Yellowstone NP to Yosemite NP to Everglades NP, as well as smaller parks. Preservationist ideals of uninhabited wilderness shaped policies of Native American removal and exclusion in the designation of national parks and the almost simultaneous development of Indian reservations, often adjacent to parklands. While the particular relationships of tribes and parklands or administrators are as diverse as the tribes and landscapes on which they lived, it is important to acknowledge that in the process of creating nearly every national park, Native American rights to ownership of lands were ignored and invalidated as these populations were pushed from their ancestral homelands, not by other tribes, as historically happened, but by the new flood of migrants from Europe, often by force or deceit.[6]

Yellowstone, as the first U.S. national park, set the stage for future efforts to protect "untouched" landscapes by excluding the Native American populations that lived on or used them. After official designation, the park's administration quickly removed the native peoples from the park to make the area "safe." The eastern press intensified calls for removal, claiming that Native Americans hadn't lived in Yellowstone previously, though twenty-six modern tribes traced their ancestral connections back to that area. The Tukudeka Tribe (also known as Mountain Sheepeaters) lived permanently on the land and considered the geysers to be sacred, and other tribes, including the

Crow, Blackfeet, Flathead, and Kiowah, used the lands at certain times during the year to hunt or gather resources. Once the land was protected and preserved as a park, Native Americans lost access to the land for critical subsistence and traditional practices.

In Yosemite, the Ahwahneechee Indians resided in and knew the region as "Ahwahnee" or "gaping mouth-like place" long before the Mariposa War of 1851, in which California soldiers "discovered" the valley while pursuing the Ahwahneechee and subsequently re-named the area Yosemite. A long and unique history of both resisting and adapting to the immigration of European-Americans into their homeland enabled tribes in Yosemite to temporarily remain on their land once it was protected. The National Park Service ultimately forced their removal in the 1930s once the presence of Native Americans in the park proved too exceptional.[7] This pattern of expulsion was often repeated for other newly established national parks.

Yet the history of Native Americans and national parks also includes commemoration and preservation—including the creation of parks such as Mesa Verde (ancestral Pueblo), Canyon de Chelly (ancestral Pueblo and Navajo), and numerous historical parks such as Casa Grande Ruins (Hohokam), Effigy Mounds (Red Ocher and Hopewell), Nez Perce National Historical Park (Nez Perce), and more. Although in recent years there has been an acknowledgment of this history by the National Park Service, as well as a recognition of the high value of traditional ecological knowledge and in some cases co-management with the tribes, much more needs to be done overall and in each park to honor the relationship of Native Americans to those lands and to work with the tribes as partners in protecting resources.

Since 1916 Congress has assembled the system of national parks managed by the National Park Service as a curious, politically driven mix of natural and cultural sites containing roughly 85 million acres (about

3 percent of the nation's total land; 1.5 percent of the land in the lower forty-eight states), in a wide range of conditions, to be preserved in perpetuity for all to seek and enjoy. This sizable acreage is spread across 417 park "units" (the unfortunate bureaucratic term) that contain a wide range of resources, from scenic wonders to culturally significant structures and landscapes.[8] Many national park units are inspirational in their natural grandeur, and a growing number are historical and often culturally thought-provoking. About 270 units have significant natural resources, including many cultural sites that also protect their natural resource context as well. The inventory of park units (identified in often confusing categories from "national parks" to "national recreation areas" to "national historical parks") reflect the range of the American landscape and the rich sounds of our place-names: Shenandoah, Congaree, Mesa Verde, Zion, Sequoia–Kings Canyon, Death Valley, Kenai Fjords, Haleakalā.

Among government bureaus the National Park Service (NPS) is fortunate to have a most dedicated if small workforce (equal as of 2018 to over 22,000 total full-time employees, but also temporary, seasonal, and part-time workers and approximately the same number of employees as the Philadelphia school district). NPS personnel are committed to the agency and its mission, often with missionary zeal. Many in the field can recite key parts of its mission as stated in the Organic Act from memory.

Some work for the NPS because childhood family vacations in national parks made a lifelong impression (as we've seen) and many others because of the NPS mission. Still others, especially in management, construction, and administration, could be equally happy in any federal agency. Ironically, only a very modest portion are technically versed in fields such as ecology or geology that deal with the key responsibility of understanding resources, especially complex natural systems.

It has always been surprising to us that in many gatherings of the National Park Service's leadership (and we have attended quite a few), entire meetings spanning days and days were spent without any mention of park resources. Visitor services, public relations, maintenance backlogs, employee housing, uniforms, law enforcement weapons standards (revolver barrel length, for example), facility construction programs and priorities, park concessions contracts and lawsuits, personnel diversity and training, and roads and road maintenance are the most frequently discussed and favored topics. Leadership, most often chosen from within the ranks, is rarely technically trained and usually uncomfortable or dismissive of science and technology. Promotion patterns have only recently graduated from the "old boy" network to "old gender-neutral" networks, with minorities recruited in an effort to convert a family vacation–derived white middle-class workforce into a more diverse one that "reflects the face of America." In our experience, most NPS employees feel that the NPS does great things for society and is poised for greater strides; many employees see themselves in roles that anyone with a social conscience and a love of nature will envy.

The overall result is an agency with hardworking, dedicated employees, well-meaning managers, and a "small-family" feel. Yet few are trained to think about or cope with the innate difficulty of saving complex natural systems in human-dominated landscapes, and too little time is spent preparing the service for the challenges of the future. In many ways the agency seems like a comfortable small family on a picnic that hasn't prepared for the storm clouds gathering on the horizon.

In this book we provide examples illustrating that national parks matter in ways that Congress could never have foreseen and that national parks are analogs for many familiar and important roles in modern society. We think that one of their most important roles may be as classrooms and living laboratories for teaching the most valuable lesson of all: that we can, and must, leave significant portions of planet earth unimpaired for wild life and for the enjoyment and environmental enlightenment of present and future generations of humans. If this mission is accomplished, future generations will stand in admiration of our resolve and in appreciation for the wisdom and foresight of the society that spawned this idea.

This argument is all the more important, because a successful outcome is less than assured. As the National Park Service enters its second century, this small government bureau is besieged and buffeted by outside forces and internal ironies and by a general failure to recognize, appreciate, and assist in the essence of its primary endeavor—the preservation of resources across generations. Not all is as it should be, and this should trouble everyone.

If the character of the nation is shaped by its natural resource heritage and the nation's character and identity are worth protecting, national parks may matter in ways we have yet to recognize, voice, and accommodate. National parks thus matter for their link not only to physical support of unimpaired life processes but also to the long-term self-esteem and psychological health of the nation. If that is true, national defense requires not only a force of arms but the forces of environmental awareness, conscious planning, design, restraint, and fidelity. If national parks are a core of our binding identity, more serious thought, struggle, and resources are required to keep the preservation of our distinctive and inclusive national identity a viable option for the future. This book is about the substance and value of national parks, what roles they now play and should play in the future, and the wide gap between image and the reality regarding the serious effort needed to protect them. We believe the challenges to the future of healthy national parks are enormous. We also believe that these are challenges that we as a people can and must master. The quality of our future will depend on how our natural heritage endures.

In the past, the National Park Service somewhat unconsciously pioneered the science and practice of dealing with limits—sustainable use balanced with enjoyment without resource impairment. In the future, the nation will greatly need the agency's mindset, practical lessons, natural systems science, management skills—and its stories.

Success in changing human society's relationship with nature is not easy to visualize. There are many barriers. Deepening inequality makes this message difficult to convey. There is likely far less appeal to limits of consumption among those who haven't yet prospered in this age of prosperity—even to the level of meeting basic needs. The message of planetary limits cannot be well received by the poorest 82 percent of the human population, which now has the benefits of only 1 percent of the world's wealth. Recent statistics show that the forty-two wealthiest individuals have *twice* as much of the world's wealth as the poorest 3.7 billion people.[9] It is basic human nature that neither the very rich nor the very poor will want to hear that an age of frugality and self-restraint is here. Problematically, there are many illustrations of how hard it is for humans both individually and collectively to move away from free-for-all materialism and resource consumption toward sustainability. Few want to accept the idea that there are limits to what we can ask of the earth; fewer still will act on it. The politics of prudence and restraint and the economics of asking less from the earth have relatively few serious champions. As one potentially powerful agent of change, the National Park Service's institutional ability as well as the federal lands context in which it operates reveals serious limitations.

We are cautiously optimistic, though. Sustainability has entered the strategic thinking of many corporate leaders, government agencies (both local and national), households, and persons. Universities and colleges throughout North America have courses and degree programs that teach sustainable practices and principles. A younger generation is emerging with a tentative willingness to turn away from mindless consumption to mindful decisions about lifestyles. As the national parks (and the National Park Service) begin their second century, revisiting their mission and role in American society and the world at large is both necessary and opportune. As we will show, the national parks are uniquely American covenants, serve important roles, and are powerful models on which to promote meaningful change.

Channel Islands National Park.
Large-scale restoration projects, like removal of the black rat from Anacapa
Island, require in-depth science and comprehensive public education and
outreach. (Courtesy of the U.S. National Park Service)

3

How National Parks Serve the Nation

Our good fortune in having careers associated with national parks is rooted in their being considered by many, including noted author Wallace Stegner, to be "America's best idea."[1] The national park idea is generally traced back to the campfire discussions and resolve of a few individuals in the 1870 Washburn-Doane Expedition, who saw the Yellowstone area as a special place that should never be despoiled— but rather protected over time and available for all to enjoy. This led to the Yellowstone Park Act in 1872. This idea has since spread around the world, with great popular appeal and positive impacts on special places in nearly every country.

Whether or not it is the greatest idea America ever had—there are some strong competitors—our experience tells us that, as great as the idea has shown itself to be, we do not yet know its full significance. The ecological implications of national parks could only begin to be understood and fully developed as the field of ecology simultaneously developed in the twentieth century. As environmental concerns rise on a global scale, we believe "America's best idea" will prove even better than we know in critical ways.

How do national parks serve us today? And what roles do national parks play that warrant the kinds of commitment, care, and expense necessary to establish them and keep them unimpaired? Part of the answer lies in their known functions—what they do for us and for nature now. Then we should consider how important they are likely to be in any future we can foresee. If there is a case to be made that parks matter in important ways that we already know about but also in ways we can only imagine, this compounds what is at stake in the fate of national parks. We must then weigh the steps and kinds of commitments necessary to ensure they can be positioned to perform those roles.

The national park idea has evolved over time. Since this evolution was beginning along with the birth and early development of the field of ecology, the immense ecological implications of maintaining natural systems within larger, problematic landscapes were not yet part of the early thinking about the purposes of national parks. This history is superbly documented in Richard Sellars's seminal book *Preserving Nature in the National Parks.*[2]

During the early history of national parks, management efforts centered on gaining popularity and hence political support by catering to the comfort and entertainment of the wealthier classes. Early alliances with the railroads explain the grand lodges in Yellowstone, Yosemite, Grand Canyon, and the other large western parks. National parks were vacation destinations.[3]

An early and powerful advocate of this entertainment role for national parks was the first director of the National Park Service, Stephen Mather. Mather was a mountain-climbing millionaire in his late forties who frequented national parks, including Yosemite, Sequoia, and Rainier. In 1914 Mather was brought to the attention of the secretary of the interior, Franklin K. Lane, as a potential assistant. Lane asked Mather to write him a letter on the current condition of the parks. Mather's letter was quite critical, including this observation: "Scenery is a hollow enjoyment to a visitor who sets out in the morning after an indigestible breakfast and a fitful sleep on an impossible bed."[4] Lane responded that if he didn't like the way parks were being run he could come to Washington and run them himself. As director, Mather and his assistant Horace Albright (who became the second NPS director) set the strategic trajectory for national park leadership. The dominant focus of park managers was to be on providing for visitor services, thereby developing a constituency among the public that would encourage support in Congress for funding the creation and operation of national parks and the National Park Service.

In large measure, this focus on man-made infrastructure in parks was successful and continues today. Early efforts to attract a constituency included staging wildlife in pens for viewing, eliminating predators so that wildlife herds would be more plentiful for visitors to view, staging fire falls from El Capitan in Yosemite National Park, providing bleacher seats for watching grizzlies feeding at the Yellowstone (and Sequoia) park's garbage dump, and so on. In the words of Bob Barbee (famous for being the superintendent of Yellowstone National Park who ably managed the wildfires when a good part of the park was burned in the 1980s), the early national parks were seen and run as "rustic fun farms."

Beyond this common goal of visitor access and enjoyment, each national park may have additional purposes or roles resulting from the mindsets of those involved in its establishment; these are often reflected in its legislative history and the enabling legislation for each park. A good example is Great Smoky Mountains National Park.

The highlands of Tennessee and North Carolina are a region containing more tree species than grow in all of Europe. By any measure, the contemporary forests of the Great Smoky Mountains are a special place where eight decades of forest protection have created a landscape that leaves a powerful impression on even the most casual visitor. Yet there was a time in America when it seemed to even make sense to cut down old-growth pecan trees in order to easily harvest the nuts. Uncut, old-growth forests were rapidly disappearing everywhere.

By the mid-1920s the Great Smoky Mountains were being laid bare. Industrial logging with steam-powered skidders had "skinned" 300,000 acres of hitherto untouched forest. Opposing this onslaught was the personal effort of Horace Kephart. He was brilliant and had entered college at fourteen but had failed in his marriage and his career by age forty-two. He found refuge and purpose in life in the remaining wilderness of the Smokies. Kephart sparked the eventual preservation of over 500,000 acres through the establishment of the Great Smoky Mountains National Park. Kephart asked: "Why should future generations be robbed of all chance to see with their own eyes what a real forest, a real wildwood, a real unimproved work of God, is like?"[5]

These lands were eventually saved through a campaign that wedded love of nature with the pennies of schoolchildren and the prospects of long-term economic benefit through park-based tourism. The alternative—ten or fifteen years of lumber-mill profits and minimum-wage employment followed by decades of economic and ecological poverty—would have left a different legacy for the nation and forever changed the conditions that had supported some of the nation's richest wild life habitat.

The idea of establishing a national park in the Smokies was of course not universally supported, as has nearly always been the case elsewhere—then as now. The timber companies raced to clear as much virgin timber as they could within the proposed park boundaries, leaving only 100,000 acres of unharvested timber by the time the "forces of evil" (as conservationists were characterized by the harvesters) could set park lands aside in 1930 for future generations.[6]

Today, the value to our nation of protecting those lands is immense in many ways. The role of national parks as drivers of local economies has become quite powerful. It should be noted here that today some of the biggest proponents and protectors of Great Smoky Mountains National Park are the chambers of commerce in the adjacent communities of Gatlinburg and Pigeon Forge. So much so that towns adjacent to the park have begun asking how they can adopt softer ways of developing and operating so that the long-term health of the park will not be undermined. The park remains the most biologically diverse in our national park system.

The Great Smoky Mountains National Park today acts as a reserve—a reservoir or a savings account—in terms of species present. While the biological community is not "complete" until certain species, such as the red wolf, are successfully restored, the park, by some estimates, may contain as many as 100,000 species of animals and plants.[7]

Once at the Great Smoky Mountains National Park's Highlands Visitors Center, a small, brightly colored caterpillar making its slow way across a stone retaining wall caught Mike's eye. Its bright, tubular body was covered in various tufts of bristles and barbs in red, yellow, and black. Though only two inches long, it had also been spotted by a young, red-haired local mom carrying a baby strapped to her chest. She stopped dead in her tracks. "Henry!" she yelled back to her husband in the car, "Come quick, it's a varmint!" Henry soon arrived, and Mike expected that Henry would quickly dispatch it—but they watched together in fascination as it inched along and eventually disappeared into the ground cover. Their fascination and reverence seemed a good omen for a park whose appeal includes the wide range of undisturbed nature, relative to and in sharp contrast with the glitzy entertainments of the nearby towns.

One of the more remarkable, if subtle, wild life displays in the Great Smokies was only recently discovered by the park staff; locals have long known about them. The show is put on by synchronous lightning bugs, "fireflies" in the North. On a warm summer's night, deep in the Great Smoky forest, entire slopes are illuminated in a giant spontaneous flash by hosts of male lightning bugs seeking mates. It is a surprisingly awesome sight. Equally surprising were the hordes of visitors who came to see them—a few in wheelchairs!—navigating old logging roads in the pitch-black night in hopes of viewing the phenomenon they had only heard of by word of mouth. Remarkably, there was an unwritten and silent pact to use their flashlights sparingly, so that these night visitors, with their heightened night vision, could wander off to see the mountainside flash brilliantly in thousands of simultaneous points of light. There was a hush and shared sense of awe attesting to their appreciation for places that harbor the smaller but great wonders of nature. The phenomenon has continued to gain in popularity such that the park now has a lottery to manage the numbers of visitors pressing to see it. Who knew?

Thus parks serve as sanctuaries for important things we often don't know about. Curiously, it was the entrepreneurial spirit of resource managers of the Great Smoky Mountains National Park that successfully launched the world's first attempt at a complete inventory of a protected area's plant and animal life—the All Taxa Biodiversity Inventory (in eventual partnership with Discover Life in America).[8] This attempt to inventory all the species in this biological reservoir is both a scientific challenge and a monumental documentation of the park's and the nation's natural legacy. The systematic search for species and the resulting massive catalog and collection of museum (voucher) specimens will be the cornerstones of tomorrow's understanding of what is in this single park, where it's found, and where the park's creatures are headed in terms of species evolution or extinction, environ-

mental health, and climate change. The All Taxa Biodiversity
Inventory, originally conceived of by scientist Dan Janzen and his
Costa Rican colleagues, is also a prime demonstration of the function
of parks in providing natural laboratories that often can be found
nowhere else.[9]

Wild and healthy national parks thus serve as reserves of the
plants and animals native to North America. These reserves provide
accessible areas showcasing the nation's natural heritage. Parks also
provide sources of wild life to replenish adjacent lands through the
natural cycles of growth and decline of plant and animal populations
in any locale. The harsh alternative would be what Thoreau wrote
about Massachusetts in his journal in 1856: "When I consider that the
nobler animals have been exterminated here—the cougar, the panther, lynx, wolverine, wolf, bear, moose, deer, the beaver, the turkey,
etc., etc., I cannot but feel as if I lived in a tamed, and as it were, emas-
culated country."[10]

We associate abundant wild life with harmony in nature
and quality of life for humans. It is an interesting study in *human*
nature that so many of our most privileged citizens, when financial
resources (or telecommuting) permit, move to the wilds of Montana
and Wyoming. They often desire to be close to a national park such
as Yellowstone. Indeed, counties bordering national parks are among
the fastest growing in today's landscape. Yet while urbanites move
to be close to nature and wildlife, it is often only a matter of a
few years, after they have planted their lawns and finished importing
exotic-plant-based landscaping, that the phone begins to ring in the
park. The recurring message goes something like this: "Please come
get your animals, they are eating my shrubs. You are maintaining a
public nuisance—keep them in the park and away from my yard or
I'm calling my Congressman." Perhaps more sympathy can be ac-
corded to ranchers who suffer losses to roaming wolves or bison, and

subsidies ought to be available to offset their need to "emasculate" their region to the levels Thoreau observed and lamented in New England.

The Great Smokies example is thus a complex and still emerging answer to the question: What are national parks *for?* This large eastern natural resource–based park, with its strong cultural heritage, acts as refuge and reservoir for wildlife, as a laboratory, carbon sink, and economic engine.

Another good example comes from Yellowstone National Park, which, along with its other wondrous natural systems and visible wildlife, maintains a nearly undisturbed geyser field. As a result of the worldwide effort to harness geothermal energy, few of the world's geyser fields have been left undisturbed. One conservation dividend from Yellowstone NP has been the protection of a rare group of organisms known as *extremophiles*—organisms that inhabit seemingly inhospitable places such as boiling-hot geysers. Extremophiles are species found in extreme harsh habitats such as undisturbed caves, glaciers, or geyser fields. A single species of microbes (*Thermus aquaticus*) found in Yellowstone's hot springs contains the heat-stable enzymes that enabled researchers to develop DNA fingerprinting, AIDS testing, and pursuit of the Human Genome Project.[11]

Some have postulated that other extreme habitats, such as those found in Kentucky's Mammoth Cave National Park, may harbor potentially medically valuable bacteria that struggle against each other for space and extremely limited food supply. To survive, they use chemical warfare against each other—the study of which might someday yield the next generation of antibiotics. That national parks and protected lands serve as reservoirs of things we often don't yet know about or appreciate suggests that they will be tomorrow's treasure troves of things that are no longer found elsewhere.

As reservoirs of the diversity of life, national parks are leaky. Many species must move and migrate. Inside park boundaries, local extinctions can occur over time due to climate change, genetic isolation, and catastrophic events. A series of favorable conditions may lead to population surges; harsh conditions can deplete populations or drive them elsewhere. Thus parks cannot be girdled—surrounded completely by inhospitable terrain (such as deforested landscapes, housing tracts, pavements, and turnpikes). Development of adjacent lands and the building of roads can have dramatic effects on the movements and persistence of native plants and animals, especially in small natural areas, making the mission of the National Park Service complicated indeed.

New England is fortunate to have a lengthy record of natural history documentation that can support long-term comparisons of trends in the presence, loss, or introduction of species. One well-studied example is a small, locally administered public recreation area, Middlesex Fells Reservation, just outside of Boston. Fortuitously there had been a complete inventory of this reserve's plant species when it was established in 1894. Beginning a hundred years later, several successive studies documented that roughly 50 of the 422 plant species had been lost, while many non-native species had been introduced. Such studies lead to interesting but difficult questions for managers of protected areas.[12]

Where the size of parks and hospitable surrounding landscapes are great enough, such parks can act as stages where the drama of natural selection can play out relatively uninterrupted by road kills and animal control programs such as culling. Large national parks, where no hunting is allowed (although a few national parks as well as preserves do allow hunting when mandated by Congress), serve as reservoirs of nature where undiminished natural selection acts on both predator and prey, determining and maintaining each other's fitness, never to be selected by the crack of a distant high-powered rifle.

When parks act as reservoirs, dramatic examples of spillover can occur when they are full, that is, home to a large wildlife population. In a future landscape that would work for nature and society, non-hunting parks would serve to support surrounding regional hunting programs by acting as supply sources producing migratory deer, elk, bison, and others. However, in today's landscapes, such as those outside Rocky Mountain National Park, where elk are abundant and highly prized by hunters, the patterns of development of lands adjacent to the park ensure that hunting opportunities are becoming limited; elk are more likely to be entangled in a swing set in a backyard than hunted. Better configuration of future land use could allow hunters to mimic the impact on wildlife population numbers once exercised by predators such as the wolf and mountain lion.

For marine parks to act as reservoirs, they must be strict marine reserves, where access to diving, snorkeling, and boating is allowed but fishing is prohibited. Healthy fish populations usually require conserving large (older) fish, which have disproportionally greater spawning potential. If these fish can be protected over their long life cycles, they can act as reserves of reproductive capacity for pelagic eggs and larvae that will recharge down-current waters outside reserve areas. Such prudent management requires an understanding of fish habitat and population dynamics—usually missing when either NPS or state fishing regulations (often in effect in national parks) are formulated. The same often goes for commercially valuable invertebrates like clams and abalone. In chapter 6 we'll see that fending off hunting and fishing pressures is but one example of the struggle to keep national parks healthy.

National parks sometimes serve as rehabilitation clinics. It may come as a shock for many who have visited the better-known national parks to learn that many units in the National Park System have serious ailments and impediments. As mentioned earlier, Gateway National Recreational Area in New York City has world-class landfills originally built and managed with no real environmental standards, to the detriment of park waters such as those in Jamaica Bay.

Similarly, there are toxic waste sites and abandoned mines (including mine shafts and strip mines) in many of the western parks. Clear-cut redwood forest areas included in Redwood National Park are slowly recovering due to substantial effort and investment by the National Park Service. There are also many parks where important components of the animal and plant communities have disappeared. In some parks the animal populations (like the Florida panther) are so isolated genetically from other populations that without intervention their genetic health and long-term survivability will be compromised. Still other parks suffer from past development and modifications (dams, roads, seawalls, and so forth) that interrupt river flow, migratory patterns, or dynamic processes like barrier island formation.

Fortunately, areas that have been brought into the National Park System with impaired resources are subject to the same policies as the rest of the system—and become, in essence, environmental health research laboratories. Driven by the implications of the Organic Act, management sometimes requires hands-on restoration by the National Park Service. The mission of the NPS forces interdiction of threats and has led to restoration efforts incorporating complex cutting-edge and large-scale restoration of both species and habitat. In many cases the National Park Service has taken on these ailments and in some cases made spectacular improvements.

A great example is the success of California's Channel Islands National Park and its partners in removing the black rat (*Rattus rattus*) from Anacapa Island at the park. The presence of the non-native rat was not unlike an infection taking over a healthy living system.

Anacapa Island is small, with steep lava rock cliffs, and is home to the rare seabirds Scripp's murrelet and the ashy storm-petrel, as well as a rare subspecies of deer mouse. It is also home to the largest breeding colony in the United States of the endangered California brown pelican. Since the introduction of the black rat, sometime before the 1940s, the rat had fed unchecked on birds and their eggs, reptiles, amphibians, and invertebrates—decimating them all.

National Park Service policies allow for direct intervention to remove exotics and protect and restore native plants and animals as part of maintaining the nation's characteristic heritage in a healthy state. In order to "first do no harm," restoration of natural conditions in complex systems requires thorough scientific understanding of the problem and identification of a workable solution. This is often time-consuming since it is done with intense documentation, public comment periods, and public meetings, but such public engagement is critical for success.

At Channel Islands, an early step was hosting a "Rat Summit" that convened the world's most knowledgeable rat experts. A draft plan was crafted that included broadcasting a short-lived rat poison from helicopters. This had to be done in the fall—when food like bird eggs and chicks was scarce and rats were hungriest. Poison-laced pellets needed to be side-broadcast to also reach the rocky cliff–dwelling segments of the rat community. Special permission to use certain baits had to be obtained from the Environmental Protection Agency. Treatments of the habitat had to be divided into two phases. Sensitive species like migratory birds, birds of prey, and native rodents required protection. The deer mice would have to be captured and held, then redistributed after the short-lived poison had deactivated. And every rat had to be eliminated.

Once the plan had been developed, numerous public outreach efforts were required to explain the approach and the various issues that might arise and also to engender public support for the complicated and possibly controversial plan. Full disclosure of all details was facilitated by the environment compliance requirements of the national Environmental Protection Act, which ensures that the public has an opportunity to understand and comment on every significant federal action being proposed. In this case, there was apparent uniform public support, and a plan was finalized.

Yet when the plan's execution date neared, there was an unexpected intervention by the "rat lobby" (who knew there was one?). The legal challenge requesting relief for the rats by relocating them was eventually overcome, and the plan was executed. It was a groundbreaking triumph by a team of park resource managers, academic scientists, and island conservationists. Every rat on the island had indeed been eliminated. (The story served as the plot for T. C. Boyle's extraordinary novel *When the Killing's Done*.)[13]

Only long-term monitoring will determine the ultimate success and impacts of rat removal, but the early responses have been dramatic. Initial results verified substantial increases in the nesting success of Scripp's murrelets and the return of the rare deer mouse into habitat it had been driven from by the black rat. The diversity of birds of prey remained the same. All indications are that the islands' natural communities were re-equilibrating. With the "infection" repulsed, the fever had been broken.

This kind of triage occurs frequently in national parks. Abandoned mine lands are being sealed and healed. Peregrine falcons have been reintroduced to Acadia NP in Maine, black-footed ferrets to Badlands NP in South Dakota; clear-cut redwood forests are being replanted at Redwood NP, goats and pigs are fenced out of the unique forests of Hawaii, and condors are flying in the wild again at Grand Canyon NP and at Pinnacles NP in California. The remarkable transformation of the Yellowstone ecosystem by the reintroduction of the wolf (with the pivotal help of the U.S. Fish and Wildlife Service and other partners), with elk herd reductions by rangers no longer necessary, is a powerful example of a system recovering many of its former attributes with the restoration of a key species. The National Park Service, by heeding the implications of the language used in its Organic Act, is becoming an authority on restoring the health of natural systems.

As well as acting as reservoirs and environmental health clinics, national parks are a diverse portfolio of unique national assets and function as our national heritage savings accounts. Such savings are a conservative hedge for ensuring the quality of our future.

The Yellowstone bison is a case in point. In an earlier and harsher time, this nation's enormous herds of native bison were shot to extermination in order to deprive Native Americans of an important source of sustenance. The complete eradication of the once 20–30 million animals was averted by the survival of a small remnant herd (around 100–200) of native bison that still survives today in Yellowstone National Park. The park's wild, genetically pure herd (undiluted with cattle genes—crossbreeding is a common practice fostered by ranchers who want kinder, gentler bison, if any at all) now acts as a bank for seeding the restoration and redistribution of the American bison elsewhere. Today the bison herd in Yellowstone thrives until it reaches levels that trigger them to migrate beyond park boundaries. Since bison were infected by cattle with the disease brucellosis in the nineteenth century, the possibility that ranchers would have to vaccinate their cattle to prevent reinfection of their herds has resulted in thousands of bison being slaughtered when they leave Yellowstone for the surrounding national forests. Ironically, some of the U.S. Forest Service lands adjacent to Yellowstone National Park were established to provide wintering habitat for bison, but cattle-grazing leases had been granted that have more political power than the bison, sentencing these living icons to periodic slaughter. Nevertheless, the park bison herd persists and thrives, and perhaps someday the central role of the buffalo in both western ecology and culture may be more widely restored, especially on Native American lands. There are some who dream that the bison might even be reintroduced into a representative sample of their restored native prairie home.

The role that parks play as reservoirs and restorers of biodiversity makes it possible to provide genetic diversity, restoration materials, and expertise as needed elsewhere. Indeed, today the NPS is systematically collecting genetic materials and storing them in national biological archives as resources for future reintroduction of important or rare species.

Parks themselves are also like endangered species in several ways. The National Park System has a number of small-scale individual parks; each one is unique, and many are at risk. Parks cut off from their former larger landscapes will decline in species richness and overall system health. Parks like Acadia NP in Maine and even larger western parks that are still too small in relationship to the life-cycle requirements of their plants and animals can become isolated by areas with incompatible uses, such as encircling housing and roadway development. Over time, many parks gradually become simpler, more unstable, and subject to catastrophic events from which they no longer have the resilience to recover. It may take heroic measures, as is often provided under the Endangered Species Act, to keep individual parks robust and biologically diverse and to maintain a healthy National Park System.

In some ways parks play a role similar to that of museums. In a sense they can serve as exhibits or "living dioramas" of untrammeled nature. They house collections of flora and fauna (though not frozen in time), as well as artifacts such as the geological features of the

Grand Canyon, Arches NP, Yosemite, Yellowstone, Mount Rainier, Crater Lake, and many more. As in museums, you may never see all of the collection, but each time you visit you are likely to see something new. In the case of natural resource–based parks, there is a seemingly infinite number of parts, holdings, combinations, dynamic states, and daily, seasonal, and cyclic patterns that can remain fresh over a person's lifetime.

Arches NP in Utah provides a good example of what may seem at first a static display of geological curiosities. The roughly 80,000-acre park contains the greatest density of natural arches in the world. Arches' fascinating geology stems from being a part of the Colorado Plateau, which receives only 9 inches of rainfall per year. Despite this scant amount of precipitation, it is teeming with life, most of which is active in the evening or at night. Among the wild life are over 270 species of birds, plus many mammals, reptiles, and amphibians. The ground is covered with crypto-biotic soil, which is actually a living "organism" made of cyanobacteria that can include lichens, mosses, green algae, micro fungi, and bacteria. The park and its arches may seem frozen in time, but the erosional forces of wind and water continuously change the landscape, and as some arches are formed, others are eroded as pieces of rock chip and cleave. All this occurs in a time frame beyond our own.

National parks play a role in supporting the arts. They present visual scenes of great beauty across many scales, from nature's immense wonders to the smallest, most intricate details in nature. Many park resources have become touchstones of our culture. Early paintings of the great western parks were instrumental in creating interest in visiting and protecting these landscapes. Yosemite National Park in California contains one of the widest varieties of plants and animals found anywhere in the United States but may be best known for its waterfalls. Yosemite Valley contains the greatest variety of waterfalls in the world. The valley has the second-highest waterfall in the world and the tallest in North America (Yosemite Falls at 2,425 feet). Yosemite Valley excels at drawing in admirers of its visual beauty, and images of El Capitan (the iconic summit) are commonly seen in our daily lives. That Yosemite's scenery is dynamic and ever-changing guarantees a lifetime of appeal.

Bryce Canyon National Park in Utah contains a colorful landscape of rock formations called *hoo doos* that were formed by erosion and freeze-thaw cycles. The place is awe-inspiring and seems to demand that one visit a second and third time. The changing sunlight during a single day creates almost unlimited variation in the views and seems to perpetually change the mood of the place.

Perhaps the most famous "work of art" is the Grand Canyon in Arizona. Within the canyon are waterfalls, rock layers full of fossils, remnants of Native American cultures, caves, and breathtaking views. The eroded rock formations are some of its greatest attractions and come in a range of colors, forms, and layers. The canyon is more than a mile deep and contains fossils dating back 1.2 billion years. Every moment is different, attracting painters and photographers hoping to capture what they see there. It is hard to imagine an equivalent art gallery.

Parks are playing a role as the ultimate zoos as well—importantly, zoos without cages. Visitors can view wild life (often mildly habituated to humans) and gain information about them, species by species—all the while enthralled and entertained. Katmai National Park and Preserve in Alaska is famous for the highest concentration of brown bears in North America. Their fishing antics during the sockeye salmon run are famous, and the remarkable close-up viewing experience is highly entertaining and very zoolike, except that the bears are not in any way constrained. Other large land and sea mammals are often present as well.

Yellowstone is famous for the largest concentration of mammals in the lower forty-eight states, including such charismatic megafauna as grizzly and black bears, moose, cougars, pronghorn antelope, bighorn sheep, elk, bison, and wolves. The park teems with fauna in all seasons, and it's difficult to spend any time in the park without seeing wildlife. Keeping curious visitors from unsafe behavior when viewing wildlife is an ongoing management challenge.

Another example is Point Reyes National Seashore in California where nearly half the bird species in North America spend at least some part of the year, making it the park unit with the greatest diversity of birds in the NPS. Point Reyes is also home to a variety of sea-dwelling mammals, including sea lions, seals, and whales.

As already mentioned, an initial role for parks was to serve as playgrounds where visitor enjoyment and pleasure was a goal. While the earlier established parks were intended for the wealthy traveler, parks today are more and more accessible to everyone, and a special category of National Recreation Areas (NRAs) was added to the National Park System to provide more access to outdoor recreation.

For example, Lake Mead NRA is a mecca for those who love water sports in the arid west. Not far from Las Vegas, it is a popular playground for visitors who frequently have had few opportunities for experience with boats and big water. Within the NPS it is famed as a training ground for water-based law enforcement skills—because of the challenges inherent in the intersection of cowboys, liquor, boats, and deep water. The park provides adventures exploring tributaries and canyons by boat, just one of the interesting outcomes of adding the category of National Recreation Areas to the National Park System.

Rocky Mountain National Park in Colorado covers a wide range of elevations, which adds to the variety of the scenery and the experiences visitors can enjoy. There are recreational activities for people with almost every interest, from scenic drives to backcountry hiking and camping. The Continental Divide National Scenic Trail goes through the park, and outdoor activities are possible in every season.

At sea level and much closer to the equator, inspirational recreational pursuits are available at Virgin Islands National Park—a tropical paradise. In addition to the beaches and clear blue waters, this small park is mostly tropical forest with appealing hiking opportunities. There is excellent snorkeling and scuba diving, as well as other water sports such as sailing, kayaking, and windsurfing. The same is true at Biscayne National Park in Florida.

Parks now, and perhaps increasingly, play roles as places of spiritual value for those of both indigenous and contemporary faiths. They are places for contemplation, reflection, and meditation in an otherwise fast-moving world. Devils Tower National Monument in Wyoming was the first national monument in the system.[14] Devils Tower has great spiritual value to Native Americans. The tower is a sacred place with power that holds cultural significance for the members of more than twenty Native American tribes, who to this day hold ceremonies there. To non–Native Americans, the tower can also be a spiritual place (of a different kind), especially for rock climbers who feel that there can be a spiritual dimension to climbing such a unique natural formation.

Another example is Denali National Park and Preserve in Alaska. Many people go to Denali to have a personal encounter with nature and end up experiencing its therapeutic effects. The park contains Mount Denali, which is the tallest mountain in North America. Some feel the mountain has supernatural energies, and many who visit Denali National Park feel that their authentic experience with nature fosters self-reflection and contemplation.

Canyon de Chelly is home to the *Diné* (often called Navajo), some of whom are living there in traditional ways. The land belongs to the tribe but is managed by the NPS as a national monument. Among the many geological and archaeological features of this striking canyon is Spider Rock, the home of Spider Woman, an important deity of the *Diné*. Designation and operation as a national monument protects many archaeological features and artifacts *in situ* (rather than in museums) and gives visitors insight and respectful access to the traditions and traditional homeland of the *Diné* people.

Parks can fill the role of fortresses where government authority and power enforce the protection of plants, animals, and ecological processes within their "walls"—the defined perimeters of each park's boundary. Protection within park boundaries has been a cornerstone of the National Park Service's success and the reason for the conditions visitors enjoy in parks today. Yet the paradigm of defense within the boundary is only part of the protection needed.

For example, Big Bend National Park in Texas, like most parks, has a well-defined park boundary that clearly delineates the area that the NPS must protect. Within the figurative walls of the park boundary, the NPS has jurisdiction to regulate most (but not all) activities. However, the modern landscape provides major challenges to such traditional ideas of park management. Significant air pollution comes from sources within the state of Texas and from Mexico, triggering legal responsibilities under the Clean Air Act that require interactions outside the park's boundary in national and international political arenas. Similarly, oversubscription of Rio Grande water along its course results in severely reduced flows along Big Bend National Park's southern border; the insufficient water supply substantially affects the ecosystems within the park. Also coming across the Mexican border each year are thousands of human migrants, who have significant impacts on park resources and engender jurisdictional contests with the Department of Homeland Security, which conducts operations (many that are impactful themselves) within the park. Ongoing and controversial construction of physical barriers such as a wall should take into account migratory wild life (including the jaguar) and potential damage to the park staff's (and park visitors') traditional interactions with the small Mexican communities along the Rio Grande.

Glacier Bay National Park and Preserve in Alaska (with over 3 million acres) is the only place in Alaska where harbor seals are protected to the point that subsistence hunting is prohibited (it is allowed in some other national parks in Alaska). The NPS has also found it necessary to place tight controls on cruise ship traffic to protect the humpback whale from disturbance and collisions in Glacier Bay. The NPS is putting more restrictions on off-road vehicles as well, to protect park habitats.

Mojave National Preserve in California is very different from Glacier Bay but plays a similar fortress role of protecting certain animal species. Mojave was designated to protect desert tortoise habitat and open space in 1.45 million acres of North America's smallest desert. Mojave contains the largest population of Joshua trees in the world and protects over 25,000 petroglyphs and pictographs. Providing fortress-like protection for these fragile lands is an exceptional facet of maintaining these places of value to our national heritage.

Parks have growing socioeconomic roles serving as "profit centers" both for government and for local communities by charging fees, paying wages, and creating "park-dependent economies" of various scales and intensities.[15]

The economy of the communities surrounding Yellowstone National Park, for example, is flourishing. These communities are some of the most robust in the western United States, with more economic diversity and lower unemployment rates than most other counties in the country. They experience continuing growth, adding new and diverse businesses. Yet elements of the communities around the park that depend on maintaining park tourism and park-based recreational opportunities can add difficulty to park management. Management decisions that protect parks by limiting certain park activities (like snowmobiling) can affect the local businesses' bottom lines and thus are often opposed by those economically dependent on ever-greater park access. Part of protecting parks must be protection from overuse, inappropriate or conflicting uses, and excessive visitor impact. Management must achieve levels of access compatible with maintaining nature in a fresh condition, not beaten down or overrun. Balancing these facets requires a range of skills and accurate, often site-specific information.

Creation of the Great Smoky Mountains National Park in Tennessee and North Carolina has fueled the development of park-dependent communities. Before the park was established, enlightened community leaders could see the economic potential of creating a national park. Since the park's creation, the communities around it have indeed continued to grow and develop. Today, the surrounding communities contain a well-known theme park (Dollywood), several outlet malls, a casino, and much more. Many of the jobs are seasonal and minimum wage, but overall, increased business opportunities and an improved economy from tourism have provided sustained benefits for the communities. Local community leaders hold the park in great esteem and pledge to approach the future in ways that favor the long-term well-being of the park and its resources.

National parks play a role as a public commons where ownership is diffuse, access is broad, and uses compete. Costs are, and should be, borne by the general citizenry rather than by intensive users and localized stakeholders.

For example, there are six towns located within the boundaries of Cape Cod National Seashore in Massachusetts. Before the National Seashore was created, the land was owned by a mix of private citizens, several federal entities, universities, and the state of Massachusetts. As the NPS took over management of the Seashore, residents were concerned about the increased numbers of tourists and development pressures that national park status would bring, and they worked with the NPS to address these concerns. Local governments implemented zoning laws and are frequently consulted before NPS decisions are made. Local citizens are represented on the Cape Cod Advisory Board, which was created to make the concept work smoothly. This kind of collaboration between the NPS and local groups has worked well. When issues arise, there will be *sturm und drang* at public meetings, but some of this is for show. After a public meeting, the loudest critics sometimes quietly approach park staff and tell them to keep up the good work, and that the national seashore has been crucial in helping save the outer Cape's unique sense of place.

Another example of parks as commons is the Santa Monica Mountains National Recreation Area near Los Angeles. Land in the recreation area is owned by private citizens, the state, and the federal government. The state is in charge of planning, and the federal government is in charge of funding. There are several parks, public beaches, and suburbs located within the boundaries of Santa Monica Mountains NRA. Because much of the land is owned by private citizens, local governments can continue to benefit from the property taxes generated. The mix of ownership and stakeholders requires both collaboration and trust—essential elements of any successful commons.

Finally, national parks play a role as national shrines (with some of them historically referred to as America's icons or America's "crown jewels"). They are rare, highly valued, and often enjoyed with a sense of both fascination and reverence. As described in most history books about the American land use experience, national parks were considered America's nineteenth-century answer to the shrines and cathedrals of Europe. Some national park units were officially declared "icons" after 9/11 and were provided with extra security.

Yellowstone is in many ways an American shrine. Yellowstone National Park is by many accounts the first and most famous national park in the world. It is famous partly for its hot springs and geysers, as it sits atop a super volcano. The park's herds of bison remain a source of wonder and awe, enshrined on the U.S. nickel from 1913 to 1938. For many the park evokes a sense of pride in and patriotism for the nation's decision to create the world's first national park. A visit to Yellowstone is in some respects an American pilgrimage.

There are other such shrines in the National Park System. Grand Canyon NP in Arizona is also one of the crown jewels of the National Park System and one of the most treasured natural areas in the world, added to the United Nations World Heritage list in 1979. Visitors come from all over the globe to marvel at its beauty. It should be noted here that it was the NPS Air Quality Program that was instrumental in fending off a massive proposed local coal-fired power plant whose emissions would have made it impossible for visitors to actually see into the canyon.

This is only a partial list of the roles of America's national parks: reservoirs, banks, museums, art galleries, zoos, playgrounds, cathedrals, fortresses, economic engines, commons, shrines, and laboratories. Mastery of the full range of potential roles for national parks is dependent on how well they are both managed and protected. These functions and services matter now and support the rationale for their high priority in the nation's political agenda in the twenty-first century. Moreover, this brief inventory does not include roles our national parks may play in the future. The future will test whether we as a nation can consciously decide that our expanding population and economy, coupled with inevitable and disruptive climate change, requires better coordination, representation, and connectivity of natural areas if we are to protect the health of nature as part of sustaining quality of life for all. Can we ensure that our lands and seascapes work for *both* nature and society as the latter continues to expand its numbers and demands for comfort? Protection is prudent, as protecting parks now helps keep our future options open.

Everglades National Park.
Patrols and within-boundary resource protection are necessary but not
sufficient in a changing landscape. The Everglades lesson teaches the need for
long-term, cumulative science. (Photograph by Charles Lee Barron)

4

National Park Realities and the
Everglades Wake-Up Call

If parks are essential heritage and the National Park System is so necessary for the ways it serves the nation, it is important to consider how national parks in general are faring. A significant part of our nation's inheritance is now vested in America's National Park System and the system's fate is in the hands of the National Park Service. Thus this tiny agency's effectiveness matters a great deal, and a candid assessment of its competence in protecting resources would be a prudent safeguard for the future.

Our system of national parks is both a marvelous success story and a high-wire act, as protecting national parks after their designation is less than assured. As the National Park Service enters its second century it is besieged and buffeted by outside forces and internal ironies and a general failure to recognize and comprehend the essence of its primary endeavor—the long-term preservation of nature amid a growing human domination of the planet. So not all is quite as it should be.

The operation of national parks in pursuit of providing for visitor use without impairment of resources has quietly amassed practical experience in the science and practice of dealing with limits—sustainable use by visitors balanced with resource health. In the future, the nation may greatly need the agency's mindset, practical lessons, science, management skills, and stories. Yet, as a potentially powerful agent of change, the National Park Service's institutional focus and low position in the hierarchy of federal agencies, within which it must currently vie for funding and influence, represent serious constraints.

As described in chapter 1, there's no place in the National Park System that illustrates the challenges and constraints of park protection in the modern landscape—and what is at stake—more ominously than the Everglades.[1]

The Everglades' watershed begins above Lake Okeechobee and dominates South Florida. Attempts to drain and carve up the Everglades had been well under way in 1947 when only the downstream third became the national park. A large portion of the "glades" just below Lake Okeechobee had already become the Everglades Agricultural Area—700,000 acres of sugar cane fields and vegetable farms. The objective in establishing the national park at the downstream end was to preserve the most intact assemblage of wildlife left—especially the colonies of wading birds whose flights had once blackened the sky. Nowhere else could this subtropical assemblage of alligators, crocodiles, snail kites, wood storks, Florida panthers, manatees, and, above all, massive breeding colonies of wading birds be found. Yet urbanization and farming were and are relentless forces closing in on the Everglades. Farming in the southern Everglades had been aided by the advent of rock-plowing, literally grinding the southern Florida limestone bedrock into "soil"; the resulting powdered "soil" is rumored to be one reason winter tomatoes in our stores up north have so little taste.

Partnered with the perverse ability of the U.S. Army Corps of Engineers to command huge budgets and devise gargantuan projects that often prove to have made things worse, cities and farmers have been successfully provided with water supply and flood control at the expense of the Everglades' ecosystem. Acting in league with local interests, the modern phase of Everglades drainage was begun in 1948 with the Central and Southern Florida Flood Control Project—a U.S. Army Corps of Engineers project of 1,000 miles of levees, 720 miles of canals, and 200 water-control structures. The national park was just one downstream fragment of a landscape now increasingly dependent on this engineered system. In reality, this national park may have been destined for failure at its outset due to historical and political realities, compromise, and honest ignorance.

By the late 1950s, water that had originally made its way down the deepest slough (no deeper than a few feet) in the eastern Everglades had been rerouted by the U.S. Army Corps of Engineers to higher elevations in the west. This provided flood control, allowing encroachment by new residential and commercial developments, including new towns. It also deprived wading birds of access to large areas of peripheral wetlands (those critical wetlands on the edges of the Everglades) that were important feeding areas at certain times of the year.

In addition, the deeper pools of the eastern Everglades had historically persisted through the dry season and been rich sources of fish. When these pools dried up and the fish were lost, the colonially nesting wading birds were forced to abandon their nests before their young could be fledged. It was a trap the birds were in no way prepared for—and not understood by anyone at the time. As successive generations of fledglings starved, the huge flocks—one of the compelling reasons for Everglades National Park's establishment—dissipated and dwindled. From historical estimates of 250,000 pairs of nesting wading birds, by the 1980s the park staff was reporting 1,000 pairs of great egrets and 500 pairs of snowy egrets. For perhaps the first time since the de-authorization of Fossil Cycad National Monument in 1957—because visitors had filched the cycad fossils—the NPS was in danger of losing its charge without much of a fight.

From the beginning, the Everglades staff did try to protect park resources—albeit in a general, arm-waving, noble-cause way. In the 1950s and 1960s, Everglades had several naturalists/ornithologists and hydrologists, but they were no match for the huge technical staffs and political backing of those who managed Everglades water flows—the South Florida Water Management District (SFWMD) and the U.S. Army Corps of Engineers. District and Corps professionals were justifiably proud of the rapid rate of suburban development in South Florida brought on by the massive dewatering of the eastern Everglades and the remarkable levels of flood control that enabled new cities and suburbs to occupy key peripheral Everglades wetlands.

The plummeting of annual bird counts in the Everglades NP signaled a problem but not much about the proximate cause and much less about the solution. Early on, park staff were asked for recommendations about what was needed to save Everglades NP. The issues were far more technical and sophisticated than the NPS was equipped to understand and address. Regrettably, the park's early recommended solutions were later proved to be just wild guesses that had actually made things worse. South Florida was a rude awakening for an agency charged with maintaining complex resources unimpaired without knowing anything much about them.

It is telling that the assistant secretary for Fish, Wildlife, and Parks coming in with the Nixon administration, Nathaniel Reed, could see things more clearly. Reed had South Florida roots and fervent conservation leanings. As an assistant secretary in the Department of the Interior, he was able to exercise some control over NPS budgets and policies. Concerned about declines in the number of wading birds, Reed approached Everglades National Park in the mid-1970s with an offer to fund a research center in the park to tackle saving—and maybe restoring—the Everglades. Everglades National Park's leadership said it was "not interested" in increased funding for that purpose.

Now it is quite rare for a park to say no to any increase to its annual budget, but tradition held strong that rangers had things, especially resource management, well in hand.

Not easily deterred, Reed approached the NPS regional office in Atlanta, the park's theoretical "boss." Again, there was no interest in his offer. Correctly evaluating these responses, Reed went back to the park with an offer they couldn't refuse. He offered the park base increases (those funds that recur automatically each year) of $1.6 million for a research center, and he threw in an additional $0.8 million increase for the traditional ranger's "hands-on" resource management duties. He had discovered the power center in NPS and bribed it. These amounts were staggering investments in both science and resource management for the NPS at that time. And his strategy worked.

But while the park accepted the research center, it really didn't much care for it. By 1989, after a decade of inflation, the South Florida Research Center's budget was still $1.6 million. Moreover, the $0.8 million had disappeared into park coffers, while all the resource management duties (the hands-on implementation work) were transferred to the center. Faced with a halving of its effective budget, the center's researchers were gradually replaced with technicians to save money. The center was housed in a snake-ridden former Cold War Nike missile military barracks deep in the Everglades (Cuba was not far away). Pygmy rattlers lived in the center, feeding on the mice that infested the ceilings, occasionally dropping down on desks when the ceiling tiles were left ajar to accommodate computer cables. The center's main entrance was fitted with a powerful fan that blew straight down over the doorway to discourage mosquitoes from entering, but half were blown away and the other half were given a jet assist directly into the front hallway. Staff came and went at a fast pace.

By the late 1980s, the center had assumed all the duties of the Resource Management Division, whose money had been siphoned off into other park priorities such as administration and visitor services. Research—the only hope of saving park resources—had been marginalized and suffocated in the nation's most imminently threatened national park. The center director position had remained vacant for several years due to a general lack of interest. Nevertheless, the small group of remaining scientists in the South Florida Research Center endured and within a decade were becoming a force for Everglades triage and restoration.

One scientist in particular, Bill Robertson, held the record for tenacity. "Dr. Bill" worked as a scientist in Everglades National Park for forty-six years (1951–97). He observed everything about the park and wrote the perfect book on the park's natural history (*Everglades—The Park Story*) in 1958.[2] Besides his long-term sooty tern studies, his most lasting contribution was perhaps his understanding of the natural role of fire in maintaining the natural Everglades. While forest fire suppression was effectively eliminating fire from its natural role in forests across the nation, Dr. Bill was proving that there would be dire consequences of the loss of fire in fire-adapted plant communities. We are seeing the same effect play out widely now, especially in the west. When Mike arrived in the Everglades as research director, Dr. Bill was among his small staff of scientists.

Shortly after Mike's arrival from Boston, the park superintendent went into Mike's office concerned about ranger reports of a die-off of patches of sawgrass in the eastern part of the park. Sawgrass is the signature Everglades plant, so this was not good news. The superintendent suspected it must be due to pollution from the local tomato farms and was considering filing a lawsuit against the local farmers. He asked for advice. Having seen sawgrass mainly from his window seat on his flight to Miami, Mike said he'd have to look into it. He found Dr. Bill and asked him what he thought. Bill was very shy and looked at his shoes as he mumbled. He said he had occasionally seen sawgrass die back in small patches over the decades, often over a several-year cycle—and it had something to do with the grass's nitrogen cycle. He called it "senescent sawgrass" and told Mike that the current die-off appeared to be a natural event, that it would probably recover the next year, and that he shouldn't worry about it. Mike was looking at his own shoes, saying to himself: "Now that's the kind of information every superintendent in every park should have access to." Regrettably, very few parks have made that kind of investment in long-term observation and understanding of their resources. Those sawgrass patches did, in fact, recover on their own. After a few years Bill and Mike became close colleagues—comfortable enough to look at each other's shoes when they talked.

By the mid-1980s the South Florida Research Center had presented a seven-point plan for Everglades restoration based on the best available science to the all-powerful board of the state's South Florida Management District. By the mid-1990s the park's South Florida Research Center had a steadily improving, science-based, model-driven understanding of how the Everglades' natural system really worked. Model development, especially for hydrological and biological systems, was key because of the massive amounts of spatial, seasonal, hydrological, and biological data that had to be synthesized. The center was aided by modelers from the Oak Ridge National Laboratory, the University of Florida, and elsewhere; Germany's Planck Institute donated their top individual-based modeler, Wilfred Wolff, for two years to work on the feeding ecology of the endangered wood stork. Everglades National Park, by way of the center, had become the driving force for a system-savvy restoration of this truly complex and compromised national treasure.

At the end of the 1980s, the South Florida Research Center had also become the key player in an audacious federal lawsuit the park superintendent actually filed against the state of Florida and its South Florida Water Management District to protect Everglades water quality. The lawsuit sought to end the violation of state water quality standards by the powerful sugar cane industry that operated in the Everglades Agricultural Area just south of Lake Okeechobee. The precedent-setting lawsuit was filed by Everglades National Park superintendent Mike Finley and the U.S. Fish and Wildlife Service's Loxahatchee Wildlife Refuge manager, Birkett Neely. Loxahatchee abuts the Everglades Agricultural Area and was receiving the brunt of its phosphorus-rich runoff. Finley and Neely had teamed up with a mercurial and controversial assistant U.S. attorney in Miami who was willing to file the unprecedented suit without asking permission from Washington. Receiving permission to sue a Republican governor during a Republican administration would have been very unlikely.

The suit correctly charged that the state had not enforced its strict water quality standards against the formidable sugar cane industry. The state of Florida had been highly touted in environmental circles for its tough water quality standards. However, receiving accolades for tough standards was one thing; enforcing them was another. Neither the state's South Florida Water Management District nor the Florida Department of Environmental Protection could muster the courage to take on "Big Sugar."

The park and refuge were ill prepared for anything but a prompt capitulation by the state. Problematically, Everglades National Park had had only one water quality technician. The compelling evidence and data underpinning the park's case actually came from the massive water quality–monitoring efforts of the state's South Florida Water Management District—the prime defendant in the suit. The district's large research and monitoring staff had collected the evidence for many years and had made technical presentations to their board and to the public that clearly documented the effects of phosphorus runoff from the Everglades Agricultural Area directly into the Everglades.

The large research effort by the district had found that farm runoff was changing sawgrass prairies (finely tuned to low levels of phosphorus) and turning them into cattail marshes (tuned to grow fast in phosphorus-rich waters). Cattails were normally rare in the Everglades. Historically, phosphorus itself had always been rare in the Everglades; almost all of it had been delivered in small doses via rainfall (around 7 to 10 parts per billion—a minute amount). Hence, Everglades vegetation is adapted to, and in fact dependent on, low levels of phosphorous. With farm runoff ten times those levels, the unique Everglades was becoming a common cattail marsh and was in danger of losing the wildlife associated with sawgrass prairies—the elements that Everglades National Park was established to protect.

Hence, the federal case was substantially set adrift when the South Florida Water Management District decided to deny the allegations and fight the suit. At the cost of millions of Florida taxpayer funds, the district hired a prestigious, aggressive Washington-based legal firm.[3] Soon the district's scientists were recanting their earlier technical presentations and even their published data, papers, and opinions. One telling declaration in the early depositions by a key district scientist was, "My opinion is: I have no opinion."

On the federal plaintiff's side, the Department of Justice first distanced itself and then reluctantly decided that the case had merit. Justice took charge and directed the park's South Florida Research Center to assemble a team of technical experts, reassemble the evidence, and prepare to spend years litigating in court.

Big Sugar watched from the sidelines—a shadow participant in the litigation. Big Sugar's strength was obviously in political power and public relations, not science. To confuse things, their tack was to publicly proclaim that phosphorus was a vitamin and therefore farm runoff was good for the Everglades, and also that the lawsuit was an example of harassment by the federal government. To shore up their claim, they searched through U.S. Geological Survey rainfall-monitoring records. Among many years of rainfall sample analyses, which showed that the rain falling on the park had averaged less than 10 parts per billion (ppb) of phosphorus, they found one sample that had registered 120 ppb—about the same level of phosphorus coming in from Everglades Agricultural Area runoff. But that one sample had an asterisk. The asterisk indicated a footnote that read, "Dead frog in collector." That one contaminated sample quickly underpinned a public relations media blitz claiming that the park and refuge were attempting to force farmers to clean up phosphorus in their farm runoff to a level much lower even than rainfall. Big Sugar's media blitz was complete with a popular bumper sticker proclaiming, "Cleaner than Rain is Insane." The park was ill equipped to overcome Big Sugar's public relations campaign that was literally intended to "muddy the waters."

What was going well for Everglades water quality and the lawsuit was largely due to the excellent assistant U.S. attorney in charge of the case. Attorney Suzan Ponzoli was more than a match for the high-priced opposing counsels, and although her efforts were largely unsung, they should gladden the heart of every taxpayer. A strong park and refuge technical team augmented by world-class experts provided by the Department of Justice drove the negotiations in favor of science and the Everglades. Early on, the federal and state opponents agreed to place their top scientists together in a hotel room and not let them out until they came up with a basic agreed-upon set of facts that might serve as a basis for settlement. State scientists gradually and grudgingly agreed (after weeks of failing the "red-face" test) that phosphorus pollution was indeed an issue and that it was undeniable that high phosphorus concentrations coming from the Everglades Agricultural Area were converting native Everglades sawgrass communities into many thousands of acres of phosphorus-loving cattail marsh. Basic science was prevailing.

Serious legal negotiations began when the tide turned abruptly in favor of the federal government due to a remarkable event in the annals of public service. At a very important pre-trial hearing—with a host of lawyers for each side, plus many more in attendance for Big Sugar—a commotion in the courtroom caught presiding federal judge William Hoeveler's eye. The newly elected governor of Florida, Lawton Chiles, had ambled in and taken a seat in front. Chiles was a lanky southern Democrat who had earned the name "Walkin' Lawton" when he won his first election by walking across the state stumping for votes. His appearance in court was a surprise to everyone, including his own legal team. Judge Hoeveler opined that he was honored to find the governor of Florida in his courtroom and asked if the governor had anything he would like to say to the court. Mike remembers the governor rising up and stating: "Your honor, I think the water's dirty. I'm here to surrender my sword. I just don't know who to give it to." He said he believed we all ought to be getting on with cleaning it up. He had apparently come up with this idea on his own, at least without warning the South Florida Water Management District's leadership or its lawyers.

The courtroom erupted with chaos at the tables of the opposing legal teams. The federal legal team was too dumbfounded to proceed with its presentation calling for a motion for summary judgment, but with the case conceded by the governor, it might well have ended then with a ruling from the bench. As it happened, it took months of negotiation before a consent decree could be drafted at the park's South Florida Research Center to end the precedent-setting federal-versus-state litigation.[4]

The ensuing celebration was short-lived. More than thirty countersuits were soon filed by the sugar cane industry against the state—all aimed at delaying the inevitable cleanup for several more years. An overall settlement was finally mediated (by a curious group of technical representatives from all parties, including Big Sugar, called "the Explorer's Group") into a settlement that included the construction of 35,000 acres of artificial wetland treatment areas. These areas would absorb the phosphorus that escaped the Everglades Agricultural Area after Big Sugar adopted stringent "best management practices" for phosphorus reduction on the farms themselves. Environmental groups wanted much more, but for the first time the sugar cane industry had to pay for cleanup costs that before had always been externalized to the Everglades.

The bold legal effort to protect one facet of a unique element of the nation's heritage had set the stage for a more comprehensive effort to restore the basic ecological processes that sustain the Everglades. The sugar cane industry had been vocal (and correct in one aspect of its defense): that water quality was only one factor in the decline of the Everglades and that the federal government should be as focused on water quantity, distribution, and timing as on water quality. The lawsuit had set the stage for a real attempt to "Save the Everglades."

After years of negotiation, compromise, and planning, political momentum to save the Everglades resulted in the "Comprehensive Everglades Restoration Plan" that is now (as of 2020) being executed, not surprisingly by the Corps of Engineers, at a cost of at least $14 billion.

As the plan slowly unfolds, the quality, quantity, distribution, and timing of water in Everglades National Park are improving. Continued public advocacy and support will be necessary to see this long-term multi-billion-dollar commitment to fruition.

Meanwhile, new challenges continue to confront the small Everglades park science and resource management staff. Extremely prob-

Everglades National Park.
Everglades restoration requires large-scale engineering projects to reverse
the harm past projects have caused. Science has been a catalyst for restoration
of the Everglades ecosystem. (Courtesy of the U.S. National Park Service)

lematic has been the importation, release, and proliferation of both invasive exotic plants and imported exotic pets that are overwhelming native plant and animal communities.

The poster villain of invasive "pests" released into the Everglades is the Burmese python. Early studies show that roughly 90 percent of the raccoons, bobcats, and opossums in parts of the Everglades have succumbed to the burgeoning python population.[5] Add to that various exotic species such as the black and white Argentinian tegu (a sizable lizard that feeds on bird eggs) and bizarre invasive fish species such as the walking catfish and Asian swamp eel, and one cannot imagine Everglades National Park wildlife as unimpaired without ongoing and upgraded heroic levels of effort. Ending participation in the international pet trade that uproots animals (including coral reef and other rare fish) from their native habitats to either live penned as pets or be set loose in places where they can do incredible harm is something valuable we all can do today.

Everglades National Park thus illustrates the enormous breadth and sophistication of challenges that can face a naive land management agency unprepared with the level of understanding and effort necessary to achieve its mission in a changing landscape. While it is the most extreme test of the NPS's ability to provide national park protection, it offers a key lesson that is widely applicable. Investment in early detection and understanding of issues combined with effective and knowledgeable advocacy can avert or lessen the damage (and ultimate costs) and achieve the intent of the park's establishment and the National Park Service's mission.

There remains scant appreciation within the NPS that Everglades National Park's management had little hope of protecting park resources until a small research center was established in the park. Or that within a decade the South Florida Research Center had collected and assimilated enough field data to devise the elements of a restoration plan that has since evolved into today's comprehensive effort that is our nation's best chance of retaining the essence and character of America's Everglades. The significance of this turnabout and the lessons that need to be learned are important not only to the NPS but also to the conservation movement.

The broad implication of the Everglades story is that the National Park Service must first do what is necessary to understand the resources under its care. The service must first invest in onsite expertise to develop this understanding. It must value science and scientists and the roles they play that lie so close to the heart of the NPS mission.

Only these essential investments will enable true protection of park resources.

Yet to date the National Park Service and Congress have not fully understood the implications of the Everglades saga for all national parks and what it will take to maintain the nation's natural heritage unimpaired. Most of what you will read about in the popular press and hear from your congressional representatives will be the need to support national parks. Usually this will mean providing funds for the built environment and its "maintenance backlog." These are infrastructure projects needed to keep the National Park System's facilities in good shape for visitors. Construction and maintenance projects are necessary for public access and popular with Congress, most administrations, and certainly the NPS. For example, when George W. Bush became president, he voiced interest in supporting national parks that was immediately translated into requests for funding for the built environment. Billions were subsequently spent on NPS infrastructure and the maintenance backlog. The irony is that no one has calculated what the "intellectual backlog" will cost (in resource loss and restoration costs) if the service does not understand what it takes to accomplish its primary mission of maintaining irreplaceable natural resources unimpaired for future generations. Parks must be more than roads, buildings, and lavatories. They must be laboratories as well.

The NPS must be able to understand the innate vulnerabilities of the natural systems in millions of acres of national parks. It must be able to distinguish imminent threats and dangerous trends from the wide variability normally found in nature. And the NPS must be able to act from a position of knowledge and credibility to oppose threats both in the court of public opinion and sometimes in hotly contested court proceedings. Over the long term, the Park Service must also be an effective teacher to ensure that its visitors and neighbors understand and speak up for the parks they love.

Yellowstone National Park.
National parks are important refuges for iconic species, such as bison, that link
us with our nation's natural heritage and enable us to remedy past missteps if
we choose. (Photograph by Jim Peaco)

5

National Parks as American Covenants

We believe that Congress, in establishing the National Park System, created a system of uniquely American *covenants*. Covenants, in the simplest terms, are what the dictionary defines as "binding agreements." National parks are covenants between the different elements of American society. These covenants are part of the "national glue" that binds rich and poor, southerner and northerner, easterner, midwesterner, and westerner. All, without regard to religion (or lack thereof), race, gender, or age, have ownership, right to access, and responsibilities under the covenants that established our national parks. These covenants, even if not fully realized, are part and parcel of the American experience.

Covenants are the essential mechanisms whereby the natural characteristics of our nation's heritage are maintained. As such, they are rightly (if not currently) above and beyond the tussles of political parties and elections. These covenants are bipartisan and even omnipartisan—Republican, Democratic, Libertarian, Socialist, and Independent—all are stakeholders in our national parks. As a goal, preservation of our national heritage transcends party differences in spite of those who would use parks or park resources as political tools to leverage temporary advantage or benefit, to unfairly profit or exploit, or to curry favor from vested interests and the powerful.

Moreover, national parks are covenants between the previous generation, the current generation, and all future generations. They are essential promises (written into law) that future generations of Americans will have the richness of these special places in an unimpaired state and accessible for their enjoyment. Not only must national parks be passed on unsullied as an inheritance to the generation that follows, but that following generation must be prepared to successfully assume their generation's role in caring for and maintaining those national park covenants—ecological, social, and political. These are grave and complex responsibilities, especially in times of rapid environmental and social change.

An Ecological Covenant

The ecological covenant and the terms for meeting it have been and will continue to be understood differently by each generation. When the first national parks were established, they were understood as places of inspirational scenery that must not be spoiled. The dynamics hidden behind the scenery were only vaguely understood, as the field of ecology was just emerging as a science. Early efforts to maintain that covenant centered on thwarting the extraction of commodities such as timber and minerals, wildlife poaching, and human habitation and development. The ecological part of the covenant was not fully incorporated into park management until much later, after many naive forays into predator control, buffalo ranching, winter feeding of bison and elk, wildfire suppression, suppression of native insects and native plant diseases, fire suppression, vista management, and broad efforts to preserve the scenery as if it were a static facade. Troubles with elk, deer, moose, and bison population boom and bust cycles gradually forced the National Park Service to seek ecologically sound approaches to park management.

One relic of this early thinking was captured in an influential study of National Park Service wildlife issues and wildlife management programs by the Leopold Commission in 1963. Among its many important insights was a vision of national parks managed in such a way as to provide "vignettes of primitive America." That vision was often translated into trying to maintain static facades of special landscapes—and freezing them in time.[1]

The concept of managing static vignettes (along with the fake narrative of "primitive America") has been discredited long since. Modern concepts of ecosystem management have been incorporated into the last several versions of the official NPS Management Policies that guide each park manager.

The current policy (as of 2006) states: "Natural resources will be managed to preserve fundamental physical and biological processes, as well as individual species, features, and plant and animal communities. The Service will not attempt to solely preserve individual species (except threatened or endangered species) or individual natural processes; rather, it will try to maintain all the components and processes of naturally evolving park ecosystems, including the natural abundance, diversity, and genetic and ecological integrity of the plant and animal species native to those ecosystems."[2]

Regardless of the burgeoning understanding of systems ecology and of its incorporation into NPS thinking and policies, the "vignettes of primitive America" paradigm had a certain appeal and still echoes in the thoughts of many older park professionals. In the face of climate change and increasing biodiversity loss, this static approach was untenable. In 2011, Jon Jarvis, director of the National Park Service, commissioned a revisiting of the Leopold Report. A high-level science committee was chartered within the National Park System Advisory Board. The committee included Gary (as NPS liaison), the former director of the National Science Foundation, two members of the National Academy of Sciences, two retired NPS scientists with outstanding careers in park science, one Nobel laureate, and others.

After a year of intense work, the committee released its report, *Revisiting Leopold: Resource Stewardship in the National Parks*. The report, widely circulated within the NPS and its stakeholder community, called for a reframed goal for NPS resource management, one that reflects a dynamic and changing world: "The overarching goal of NPS resource management should be to steward NPS resources for continuous change that is not yet fully understood, in order to preserve ecological integrity and cultural and historical authenticity, provide visitors with transformative experiences, and form the core of a national conservation land- and seascape."[3] Toward the end of the Obama administration, the NPS formally adopted this goal as part of a major policy transition (more on this later). The policy, known as Director's Order 100, became the first NPS policy rescinded by the Trump administration as part of its assault on conservation.

The ecological covenant includes preserving natural processes like fire and natural selection. The latter requires protecting species diversity and at times critical populations so that they themselves sort out ecosystem function. This includes ensuring that natural systems maintain their natural resilience to withstand significant disturbances such as periodic droughts, floods, and storms as well as climate change.

The ecological covenant requires each generation to fulfill its commitment to providing the kinds of protection necessary to confront the full range of challenges of its times. Each age has had its challenges to the covenant—from the need to control the poaching of wildlife and timber (which required enlisting the U.S. Cavalry) through World War II's need for resources, the Great Depression's need to fuel economic recovery and put people to work, and the Cold War arms race's thirst for uranium. Along the way there have been periodic successes not only in protecting park resources but also in reversing declines in air and water quality affecting parks on a regional scale. Today's challenges include the onslaught of overfishing with new technology and the increasing global quest for protein, fire danger from a long period of misguided fire suppression, prolonged droughts, global trade and the accelerated dispersal of invasive plants and animals (such as the release of Burmese pythons in the Everglades), and the deadly challenges of fences, highways, wind farms, and cell towers that add to the already precarious world of migratory species. Overall, the problem is simply that we are using nature at a rate that far exceeds its ability to renew itself. And at the top of the list of all current challenges is, of course, the joker in the deck—climate change.

Patrick Gonzales is an NPS climate scientist based at the University of California, Berkeley. Highly skilled, productive, and imaginative, Dr. Gonzales has served as a lead author for the Intergovernmental Panel on Climate Change, testified before Congress, and carefully studied climate change in national parks. His research documents the impact of rising sea levels, increased temperatures, the changing onset of plants' flowering, and the cascading consequences of this global threat to individual parks.[4]

Even with these troubling findings there is good news. Our experience indicates that stewardship by the National Park Service, with the support of preceding generations, has achieved a national park system that is generally healthy overall, with many units having been restored to conditions better than when they were brought into the system. Developing an understanding of natural system dynamics and restoring habitat health can maximize resilience and will be the best hedge in the face of climate change. Fortunately, if the NPS operates based on its growing understanding of the resources it manages, the National Park System will be on a trajectory compatible with its best defensive strategy for global climate change.

A key challenge accruing over past generations and into the present is the lack of a fully representative assemblage of protected American landscapes. To fulfill the terms of a covenant that passes on the nation's heritage to each succeeding generation, there should be a representative sample of that heritage within the National Park System.

The current process for identifying and establishing national parks has been increasingly politically driven over decades, which has affected the kinds of units added to the National Park System. Valiant and patriotic actions and sacrifices have always been necessary to counter the political tendency to establish parks only where it has been easiest and short-term economic gains are not to be had.

The result has been an impressive system, but one weighted toward rugged terrain (mountains and glaciers, for example). Other crucial habitats that are more easily developed for economic purposes are underrepresented. Perhaps the best example is the American prairie. Of the once 170 million acres of tallgrass prairie, only a small percentage remain, and only a vulnerable token representation of roughly 12,000 acres is protected within the National Park System, at Tallgrass Prairie National Preserve in Kansas. In order to establish the preserve, Kansans set a cap of 180 acres to be under NPS jurisdiction; at the present time, the NPS owns only 35 acres in the preserve.

Similarly, southern bottomland forests are missing from the system and are at great risk. One outstanding example, championed for inclusion by the eminent biologist E. O. Wilson, is the Mobile-Tensaw Delta in Alabama. This area is a competitor for the most biologically diverse natural system in the United States. Roughly 260,000 acres in size, for decades it has been proposed, considered, and opposed as a grand addition to the National Park System. It is a magnificent asset, and some parts of it are protected, but of course the rest is coveted by many vested interests. As we will see later, the Mobile-Tensaw Delta is an area that our foremost scientists would advise should be protected as part of America's heritage.

There are a number of other breathtaking candidates for inclusion in the National Park System that are both intact and politically feasible to include should there be the political will to try. Yet many park advocates are resigned to the perceived impossibility of adding new national parks (other than small historical sites or those that are culturally or politically significant) because of hostility toward federal land ownership among many citizens, especially (and surprisingly) those otherwise self-identified with strong patriotism.

Mike recalls the bold CEO of Parks Canada, Alan LaTourelle, saying at the turn of the millennium that Canada was endeavoring to substantially increase the size of its national park system "because we may be the last generation of Canadians that can." He was acknowledging the rapid changes in today's landscape and the universally accelerating difficulty of preserving significant portions of national heritage in the face of population and economic pressures.

If our public and our national leadership understood and chose to fully honor the ecological covenant, they would call on the National Academy of Sciences to survey the current representation of America's natural heritage in the National Park System and recommend those natural features and systems necessary to create and pass on a representative and resilient National Park System. This was one proposal of the Second Century Commission in 2009—as well as the more recent *Revisiting Leopold* report of 2011—and it remains an important task for today's leadership.[5]

The ecological covenant also demands that we use all means possible to protect what is already in our National Park System. Most importantly, each generation must follow the precautionary principle and be very careful in taking any action that might lead to irreversible impacts. Again, the NPS Management Policies reflect this fundamental principle: "In cases of uncertainty as to the impacts of activities on park natural resources, the protection of natural resources will predominate. The Service will reduce such uncertainty by facilitating and building a science-based understanding of park resources and the nature and extent of the impacts involved."[6]

Global warming predictions include those of massive shifts of species as regional weather patterns and temperature regimes change. As species shift their ranges to adapt, some may leave national parks over time and find themselves in less protected areas. When those areas are under the jurisdiction of other federal agencies (typically in the west, where 70 percent of the land is federal), new mechanisms to facilitate land swaps, co-management, and shared planning seem logical ways to maintain protection for important species. Smarter orchestration of federal lands can be an effective way to mitigate both the impacts of climate change in national parks and the nation's natural heritage in general.

Coordination of the use and management priorities for federal lands is becoming ever more important. Federal land management agencies often pursue their mission single-mindedly without regard to compatibility with either the missions of other agencies or the overall national heritage. A recent example would be the U.S. Forest Service's facilitation of a proposal for a huge upscale residential development near the Grand Canyon. Public outcry and the lack of adequate water supply in the region appear to have defeated this bad idea. But it illustrates that even the covenant protecting perhaps the most recognized and emblematic natural heritage icon in America can suffer from the actions of "sister" agencies that can potentially lead to the encirclement of currently protected areas or the interdiction of water supply and the decline of a national park.

Of course not all nationally significant heritage lands can or should be considered for federal management. As yet largely unharnessed for conservation is the latent but widespread power of the willing and committed private owner. There are many property owners who feel and act strongly out of love for nature and its expression on their lands. The land trust movement is an extraordinary testament to private owners' devotion to nature in lands they own, love—and want to see protected. Through conservation easements, different degrees of land protection can be carefully delineated in deed language that binds present and future owners. The actions of willing private landowners as a complement to the protection given by federal, state, local, and nonprofit landholders can make a critical difference in creating a connected landscape that works for all species.

The NPS National Natural Landmark (NNL) Program is a tiny program within the National Park Service that attempts to officially recognize that powerful force that is love of place, as well as the role private owners can play in keeping the diversity of habitats available and flourishing for plants and animals. The NNL program officially recognizes those owners who voluntarily enter into a covenant to maintain nationally significant natural history features that occur on their lands. The National Natural Landmark designation is nonbinding and can easily be revoked by the owners—but most aren't. Today the more than 600 official landmarks are an incredible trove of our nation's best natural treasures, whether they be waterfalls, extinct volcanoes, meteor craters, caves, bogs, swamps, or dinosaur tracks. The NNL program is a conservation bargain—it's managed by just a few employees who keep track of the program and provide advice and services to landowners as requested.

And the NNL program is a balancing act. Problematically, early on some conservationist groups looked to the natural landmarks as possible sources of future park designations (and possible "takings"), nearly killing the NNL Program politically. Pressure from property rights groups has put the entire NNL Program on the chopping block several times, but recently revised program regulations provide stronger landowner protections so that new landmark designations are occurring once again. The last time the program was suspended indefinitely by a group of Republicans in Congress, it was revived by a Republican constituent working with California Republican governor Arnold

Schwarzenegger. This program and others that encourage the conservation of private property, while carefully protecting landowner rights, can be enhanced as an effective way to harness the motivation of private landowners toward furthering the nation's conservation and national heritage goals—without additional federal ownership of lands.

In 1961 Cape Cod National Seashore was established in an area that had already been inhabited since early colonial times. Only through working with well-established and tradition-bound local towns and by accommodating private inholders (those owning property inside a park boundary) in many cases was it possible to have a nationally protected area in such an expensive and inhabited location. The "Cape Cod Model" of park creation was an ingenious breakthrough for working to protect lands of great scenic and ecological value that had been inhabited and developed for three hundred years and were at great risk of rapid and intensive development.

Such success is neither easy nor assured. Among Cape Cod's local traditions and practices were some that could not continue if natural resources were to be unimpaired. On Cape Cod, the local County Mosquito Control Board is a powerful political force. It is responsive to constituents, claims credit for controlling insect-borne diseases, and gains great favor by responding to complaints about nuisance mosquitoes. The local tourism-dependent economy supports the control of mosquitoes and greenhead flies at practically any cost.

However, having a national seashore as a neighbor can lead to minimizing the ecological impacts as well as examining the cost-benefit ratio of traditional practices. In this case the Seashore staff needed to know if the county's mosquito-control practices had significant impacts on wetland ecology within the Seashore and to what extent they were effective in the control of mosquitoes.

Mosquitoes often made the phone ring in Cape Cod Seashore headquarters. It might be someone like the Wellfleet widow of a former ambassador and Cabinet member. In the 1970s she regularly called to complain about mosquitoes and wanted more to be done by the Seashore to provide her some relief. Her summer cottage was in the middle of the Herring River salt marsh—a mosquito's natural home, of course—yet her cottage had no window screens! Moreover, things were afoot in the Herring River that were making the mosquito issue worse.

In the late 1970s, a caller reported a massive die-off of American eels in the Herring River. As the situation was investigated, this die-off turned out to be the result of a long history of large-scale meddling with the salt marsh ecosystem.

Prior to 1906, the annual migration of herring in the Herring River was a welcomed and profitable event. Proceeds from the annual catch from the herring run covered the costs of town government. Nevertheless, in 1906 a dike was placed at the mouth of the river. The dike was fitted with a one-way flap-valve to let freshwater out of, but not let saltwater into, the river's tidal marsh. The idea was to dry the area out to enable farming while at the same time eliminating mosquito habitat. However, neither farming nor the elimination of mosquitoes ever materialized. Sadly, the dike did extinguish the annual herring run and the town's income from it. And while the marsh did periodically dry out, the number of mosquitoes actually increased, with freshwater species replacing salt marsh species.

To combat the new freshwater mosquito onslaught, it was thought necessary to further enhance drainage by digging a system of drainage ditches upstream of the dike. Ditching for mosquito control accelerated drainage and further desiccated the marsh's marine sediments that had been isolated above the dike. And this turned out to be a problem.

Diking and mosquito ditching caused the old sulfide-rich marine clays to dry out. Drying allowed oxidation of the sulfides to sulfates.

With an influx of rainwater, the sulfates formed sulfuric acid, which leached from the clays into the river. The eels began dying when the ditches had just been "cleaned" by massive digging with a large back-hoe, which had increased the exposure of sulfides and the flow of sulfuric acid. Investigation of the eel kill showed pH levels of as low at 3.5—an acidity level toxic to fish.[7]

This chemical process in clays is called *katteklei* formation and is typically found in the reclaimed *polders* of the Netherlands—where farmland has been created by diking out the sea. The oxidation of iron sulfide (pyrite) is also the basic reaction producing acid mine drainage that flows from abandoned deep and surface strip mines in coal country.

Investigations found that there were no fish left in the Herring River (except for one small bluegill found hiding upstream in a small unditched tributary). There were, however, hordes of acid-tolerant mosquitoes—*Aedes cantator*—commonly known as the "strip mine mosquito." Further, arrays of mosquito traps showed movement of those broods into the town of Wellfleet. Wellfleet had not only killed its herring run—its golden goose that had covered the town budget year after year—but also turned the results into sources of additional vexation.

Applying its management policies, it has taken Cape Cod National Seashore decades to convince the town to remove the dike and restore the Herring River basin. One ongoing delay stemmed from local reluctance to risk flooding the number 9 hole on Wellfleet's golf course. Nevertheless, with the steady pressure of policies for unimpaired resources and patient outreach to stakeholders, these wetlands—so important as nurseries for offshore fisheries and the health of a complex system of native species—are soon to be restored. If successful, the restoration will be evidence of this generation's effort to honor its commitment to Cape Cod National Seashore's ecological covenant.

A Social Covenant

One day in a taxi on the way to Capitol Hill, Mike and a colleague were discussing forest management issues related to a request to salvage "useless" trees killed by an endemic disease in a western national park. Ecologically, dead trees are valuable in many ways and not at all "useless." Bacteria, fungi, worms, boring beetles, ants, moths, butterflies, and birds of all kinds depend on dying and dead trees. And dead tree material becomes part of the soils and forest litter that support a healthy forest.

In the midst of this conversation, the turbaned cab driver turned in his seat and said, "I am a new citizen saving to buy a filling station; my son wants me to take him to a forest. But I do not own a forest." It was with great pride that Mike could say to him: "Oh yes, you do! Prince William Forest Park is just down the road, and you and your son are rightful owners and most welcome there." Mike went back to his office and designed an *Owner's Manual for New Citizens* (about the size of a Volvo owner's manual) to hand out at the naturalization ceremonies that are frequently held in national parks. It is important that it not take long for all new citizens to discover their national heritage. The power of the national park idea is that the unique and irreplaceable lands and waters in national parks are owned by the citizenry—not the federal government, not the bureaucracy, but all of us and our nation's present and future children.

The social covenant of the national parks proffers both great reward and somber responsibility for citizens as owners. The covenant requires responsible use by the current generation and accountability for the condition of the parks as they are turned over to the next generation of owners.

Relatively few of us are aware of, or in step with, the social covenant of national parks. Remember that most Americans cannot distinguish between a forest ranger and a park ranger if asked. Yet there is a continuing long tradition of awareness, use, and support of national parks by the upper and upper middle classes that goes back to when the first parks were inaccessible to many. The early national parks primarily provided opportunities for access only for those with greater means with a social or cultural proclivity for nature and wild places. The recent development of the National Park System with units in the vicinity of cities and in recreationally popular places has broadened those opportunities for access and thereby broadened the audience for and constituency of national parks. It is particularly important that all Americans benefit from the social covenant that national parks represent.

A subtle but potentially insidious threat to the idea of a social covenant may be the apparent erosion of will and vision becoming fashionable with those who see the earth as a large human and sometimes "rambunctious" garden. "Conservation science" means many things to professional ecologists, and recently a new concept of conservation science has been proposed, having as a key goal the improvement of human well-being through management of the environment.[8] This concept recognizes and accepts human domination of the planet and largely dismisses any remaining hope of retaining sanctuaries of pristine nature. With this perspective it becomes fair game for humans to consciously endeavor to shape the earth to their liking while somehow maintaining, of course, the natural processes that allow humans to persist in the first place. This "postmodernist" trend, if applied to wilderness areas and many national parks, will give great comfort to those who would open the floodgate of human demands and uses on the relatively small percentage of unspoiled nature still intact on earth. The biggest threat to the NPS covenant may well be a greater willingness to redefine its terms and goals and lower the bar in search of human comfort and profit as suggested in this "intensive interaction" approach.

National parks are the antithesis to this concept, as lands and waters brought under the purview of the Organic Act and the NPS Management Policies will be not only vigilantly protected but also returned to natural conditions—and rescued from human disturbance insofar as realistically possible. The policy of healing impaired systems is important because it signals an effort to recover an authentic experience of unimpaired nature. The policy of action to maintain or recover natural system integrity may well be the best long-term defense against the overriding influence of human activity. Restoring natural systems by returning extirpated species, controlling or eliminating invasive plants and animals, and reducing air and water pollution builds system resilience and may also be the best response to climate change in national parks.

The NPS management role includes "social stewardship," refereeing among differing and sometimes conflicting social agendas while fulfilling the terms of the ecological covenant. In practical terms, it often means saying no to a wide range of interests and wants. With over 300 million visits per year (representing an estimated 100 million visitors per year), the units of the system also represent a powerful platform for reaching the American public with messages that promote social cohesion—especially a uniform appreciation of the context of our national identity. We hope that park visits that provide reliable information on the social covenant can ensure that it is kept.

To meet tomorrow's environmental challenges with a united societal effort, national parks must become much more than vacation destinations. While retaining that popular role, as well as that of providing inspirational and spiritual renewal for so many, national parks can also become central hubs of education, lifelong learning, and community dialog. The mission of the National Park Service may not be achievable without a powerful education effort that teaches visitors and others about ecological sustainability and adherence to the social covenant through which past generations have conveyed unimpaired national parks to this generation. Only serious attention to this can ensure that the social covenant is passed on to future generations. National Park Service management must be much more nuanced than simply caretaking park facilities and refereeing among park uses and users.

At a National Parks Conservation Association dinner in 2003, Mike remembers educator David Sobel saying that national parks reminded him of foreign embassies. He said they were obviously heavily guarded and well-cared-for outposts and that there was definitely something going on inside; yet they seemed aloof and uncommunicative—and never sent anyone out much to talk to the locals. We can be thankful that his observation has become less and less true as new generations of park superintendents better and better understand the importance of public involvement in successful park protection. Yet while national parks have come a long way in positive engagement outside their boundaries, the NPS must adopt an even stronger role in educational outreach and community engagement to fulfill the social covenant.

Messages about national parks and what it takes to keep them robust and unimpaired must be rooted in each park staff's having an authoritative understanding of the park's resources. This is necessary at all levels, from interpreters giving talks to those documenting ecosystem health trends and threats.

In the past, the NPS invested in careers for park naturalists. As long-term natural history "experts" they accumulated an intimate knowledge of their parks and could speak authoritatively to visitors and neighbors on what they might see in the parks' natural world and explain what it meant. Park naturalists had long-term, four-season information that often piqued the interest of visitors and inspired many to want to learn more—and perhaps even to learn habits of observing and understanding nature more deeply themselves. But following trends in the education world in the early 1970s, this investment was scrapped in favor of hiring seasonal employees trained as good communicators.

With park naturalists consigned to history, most interpretation is now done by "seasonals" or, more recently, by amateur volunteers. At first, a summer seasonal was usually a public schoolteacher who was comfortable with science and returned to the same park year after year. Then, as the school year lengthened, as did the busy summer season in many parks, high school teachers were gradually eliminated because they could no longer sign on for the full summer visitor season. The net effect has been a simplification of park interpretive programs, often now proudly described as targeted to the "discovery" level. That usually means just a few weeks of superficial training for the newly hired seasonal interpreter, who then goes out to share natural history basics with visitors. That may suffice for a significant portion of contacts with the public, but it likely does not inspire a new generation of park visitors toward science-based conservation and commitment to the social and ecological covenant. This is a problem because the complex issues facing parks require that the public at large become sophisticated supporters who understand the implications and stakes for park protection in a human-dominated landscape.

Certainly at parks like Acadia NP, where studies have shown that a large fraction of visitors have college and post-graduate degrees, the intellectual cupboard can be a bit bare. On a nature walk at Acadia recently an earnest young seasonal cheerily informed park visitors about the "glacial morass" dominating the landscape farther south in New England. A voice in the crowd volunteered that while there might be a "glacial morass" farther south in Washington, D.C., it was a "glacial moraine" that shaped Cape Cod as well as other features in New England's signature glaciated terrain. It will take an upgraded outreach effort to strengthen support for the social covenant and create an informed public that has the understanding and resolve necessary to tackle park protection issues in the park landscapes of the future.

One experiment in responding to the need to enhance the education function of the national parks—and thereby strengthen support for the social covenant—is the NPS Research Learning Center Network. It has been built on the experience Mike had in his first summer as a researcher at the Cape Cod National Seashore. Summer housing and work space on the cape is very expensive, as it is during the tourist season in most parks. Such high housing costs are beyond the means of most field research budgets. In the summer of 1975, a group of University of Massachusetts researchers got permission from the Seashore to use an abandoned park building—called the MITRE site. This hangar-like structure had been abandoned after it was used for radar research during World War II. It provided quick access to research sites, and the researchers decided they could live there with a few amenities, starting with some two-by-fours and drywall. They hired a cook, added basic appliances, and lived communally for the summer. This arrangement worked superbly, with the one exception that the cook ran off with the district ranger.

Working at the Seashore, researchers noticed an important phenomenon. Seashore visitors frequently "mobbed" them, asking questions, expressing interest in their research, and regularly volunteering to help even though they were on vacation. Visitors frequently wanted to know why researchers cared about what they were doing and finding. Here was a sign of innate human curiosity about nature that the NPS must harness for its future success.

That summer's research set the stage for new off-road vehicle regulations at the Seashore that have since saved the magnificent dune system of the outer Province Lands. Some of the fundamentals of the dynamic nature of barrier islands were worked out that summer by Professors Paul Godfrey and Steve Leatherman, and these fundamentals have since been applied to National Park Service policies and implemented in the management of coastal parks and seashores nationwide. That summer also provided a management agenda for preserving the water quality of the Seashore's beautiful kettle ponds— groundwater-filled depressions formed by blocks of ice left by the retreating glaciers. For a relatively tiny investment, much usable knowledge was gained by Cape Cod National Seashore and indeed by the NPS as a whole.

The real payoff came later, when Mike found himself in Washington. At the time Congress was pressuring the service to either use or demolish the large inventory of unused buildings in national parks. Deputy Director Deny Galvin was convinced by Mike to propose to Congress a pilot program to adaptively reuse historic or surplus buildings as research laboratory and bunkhouse spaces. A plan for thirty-two Research Learning Centers (RLCs) across the National Park System was developed, and Congress funded twelve in the first year. RLCs were to accommodate researchers ("bait them in") and, in return, ask only that the researchers share their findings and find ways to interact to satisfy some of the visitor curiosity they were likely to encounter. Such interactions might take place in activities including guided tours or hikes, campfire presentations, science cafés, citizen science opportunities, brief courses, or seminars. University scientists seeking locations for their sabbaticals were especially sought, and the NPS experimented with a Sabbatical in the Parks program.

The immediate goal of this new dimension in park outreach to the research community was to increase the knowledge base for making park management decisions. Each RLC is a tangible long-term commitment to convening and catalyzing science-based conservation on a regional scale. The long-term goal was to build a stronger local, regional, and national constituency for fulfilling the National Park System's social covenant.

Regrettably, the budget request for the second year (2002) for twelve more centers came to the attention of the secretary of the Interior, Gale Norton. Her staff told Mike that she did not want to see parks creating another generation of "tree huggers." She redirected the second-year's increase for twelve more RLCs to the Exotic Plant Management Team program, which created circuit-rider teams that helped control weeds, mostly in western parks. Nevertheless, seven parks quietly found funds to build their own centers so that the resulting Research Learning Center Network grew to nineteen RLCs. These centers, where they remain supported by their parks and by local partners, are becoming bustling intellectual hubs. Today researchers, citizen scientists and naturalists, and local schools and organizations are finding support and a chance to join a vibrant community centered on both regional scale and park conservation. At their best, they engage the public in community science, with volunteers participating in citizen science research projects, act as conveners for discussions and debates on key environmental issues, and serve as liaisons with local-, state-, and national-level educators in science, technology, engineering, and mathematics (STEM) programs.

Where RLCs have sufficient capacity for hosting educational events and longer-term immersion in the park environment, transformational experiences can build the national park constituency in powerful ways. Acadia National Park's Research Learning Center, operated in partnership with the nonprofit Schoodic Institute, occupies a retooled former U.S. Navy base on the scenic Schoodic peninsula. It now has an overnight capacity for nearly two hundred participants. The park's Schoodic Education Adventures program operates there and brings students from Maine, New England, and New York on several-day excursions for immersion in a spectacular rocky Maine coast setting. Schoodic has hosted Maine kids who had never seen the ocean and New York City kids, forced from their secondary school by Hurricane Sandy, who had never before seen stars in the night sky. Learners of all ages find citizen science projects, lectures, courses, and festivals at Schoodic that expand their Acadia National Park experiences in life-changing ways. Participation in a community science project and learning to systematically make observations in nature can help citizens navigate a changing world and one with often conflicting streams of information.

Research learning centers are as different as the national parks that host them but represent an experiment in community outreach and in deepening the public's intensity of connection and commitment. Providing opportunities for deep citizen engagement in national parks may be the best hope for sustaining their social and ecological covenant.

A Political Covenant

The original American idea of a national park, and then of a national park system, was inspired but also naive, vague, and untested as to its staying power in the rough-and-tumble politics of that generation and era (the early twentieth century). To some extent, the same has been true of the politics of every generation of Americans thereafter. In a fashion similar to the challenges that face each generation's ability to keep the parks' ecological and sociological covenant, each generation inherits and shapes its own political atmosphere, which must be supportive of the covenant if parks are to remain protected.

Because it conserves resources in place, the National Park Service lacks the guaranteed support in Congress enjoyed by agencies that control commodities such as timber, grazing leases, mining and mineral leases, hydropower, and municipal and irrigation water supply.

Hence, a politically engaged and vocal public constituency for national parks is vital. As noted earlier, it is evident in the early writings of National Park Service leaders that building a public constituency by developing visitor facilities and services was a foremost necessity. A committed public constituency reinforces the political will.

Even with a high level of public approval of the National Park Service, NPS funding has always been seen by some in Congress as a luxury, and its budget an afterthought, when in competition with these other commodity-oriented interests. The reason is simple. In 2019, there were 11,862 active registered lobbyists—22 lobbyists for each member of Congress.[9]

Having a legacy of weak budgets and bare central office staffing in Washington puts the National Park Service among the stepchildren of Washington-insider power politics. Roger Kennedy, former NPS director (1993–97), observed that NPS support is "a mile wide but an inch deep." The implication was that diffuse popular support is often not as effective, vigilant, or focused in D.C. politics as is concentrated vested-interest pressure.

Yet by making parks accessible to a widening constituency, the Organic Act and its implementation have been largely upheld for a hundred years. Indeed, it has been strengthened substantially by some generations through supportive laws such as the Redwoods Act of 1978. That act reiterated the unimpairment standard for measuring success and the principle that no NPS activity can be allowed that would be "in derogation" of park resources and values. Thus Congress has—so far—generally maintained faith with the intent of the Organic Act and been inclined to do so because of the broad, if diffuse, reverence for national parks held by the American public.

This enduring support has slowed the rollercoaster of demands that sometimes parallels the philosophical swings accompanying each new administration and its benefactors. An example of ongoing political challenges would be certain western states' laying claim to public lands. Utah regularly attempts to assert, either legally or by direct action, the state's right to develop roads and rights-of-way over federal lands, including national parks. The state of Arizona has attempted to take over the management of Grand Canyon NP during times of budgetary crisis in Washington—and government shutdowns that close the national parks to visitors have caused both bureaucratic and political mayhem. States frequently challenge the park service's right to manage wildlife in national parks; they have been largely unsuccessful so far. With the election of Donald Trump and his appointment of Ryan Zinke as secretary of the Interior, followed by oil lobbyist David Bernhardt, another cycle of challenge to the National Park System has begun. On his first day as president, Trump called the acting director of the NPS (Mike Reynolds, an excellent career NPS administrator) to berate him and the NPS for allegedly minimizing the crowd size of his inauguration. It was not a good omen. Gary and former NPS director Jon Jarvis (in their book *The Future of Conservation in America: A Chart for Rough Water*) have documented the Trump-led assault on conservation.[10]

National parks are quintessential expressions of American confidence in the future, and the ecological, social, and political obligations that, combined, create this distinctive American covenant are vital to our nation's future. So far, the mission of national parks has almost always been better defined, extended, and upheld by each generation. But this can never be assumed.

Black Canyon of the Gunnison National Monument.
Protecting processes such as the erosion cycle in Black Canyon is part of the
National Park Service mandate, often threatened by sharp changes in political
agendas. (Photograph by Lisa Lynch)

6

Navigating the Future: Perils and Opportunities

Theodore Roosevelt had the right idea on July 4, 1886, when he said: "We have fallen heirs to the most glorious heritage a people ever received, and each must do his part if we wish to show that the nation is worthy of its good fortune."[1] If national parks are covenants between all Americans—within and across generations—then it is essential that each generation understand and address the perils that America's national parks will encounter on their watch. Each generation's legacy can also be one of seizing opportunities as they arise to keep, enhance, and perfect the American covenant embodied in our National Park System.

Perhaps today's most perilous factor is the state of public awareness. This ranges from the larger issues down to the small. While national parks have many devotees, most Americans do not distinguish between national park rangers, U.S. Forest Service rangers, U.S. Fish and Wildlife Refuge managers, and state and county park rangers. While the lack of differentiation among agencies with different agendas is understandable, it doesn't bode well for the future of the strict nuances of the unique mission of national parks. When difficult environmental issues arise or support for establishing a new national park is needed, understanding the very real differences among agencies and their approaches to land and resource management is crucial.

National parks are usually considered among our most stringently protected lands, with exceptions such as the Wilderness Areas that are also found in the U.S. Forest Service and Bureau of Land Management areas. There are other rare instances in which state parks (like Baxter State Park in Maine) are more restrictive than most national parks. Restrictions may irritate special-interest groups such as jet skiers, snowmobilers, off-road vehicle enthusiasts, hunters, trappers, fossil collectors, mountain bikers, and others, who press for fewer limitations and greater access. They can find fewer restrictions on Bureau of Land Management lands (some 248 million acres—almost entirely in the west) and those of the National Forest Service (193 million acres, mostly in the west, but also three-fifths of federal land in the east). The Fish and Wildlife Service manages 89 million acres, of which 77 million are in Alaska, and it is somewhat less restrictive in many ways but certainly so regarding hunting and fishing. Also, national parks often have special uses built in by their enabling legislation, so that one can find most activities somewhere in the National Park System.

The demanding mission given to the National Park Service over the long term will require the most idealistic and careful balancing act, as well as cooperation from both private and public sectors, to achieve unimpaired heritage protection. Each generation must learn about and understand the special environmental and social conditions that determine both peril and opportunity in its time of stewardship. Not only will the perils and opportunities be different for each generation; the actions required of each generation to fulfill this unique American covenant will be distinct. As in the past, though, it is likely that the best strategic approach is aggressive action in seizing opportunities for full heritage preservation and, where necessary, restoration, while mounting a determined defense against all perils.

It is an interesting question as to which era of National Park System history has presented the greatest peril or the most difficult sociopolitical and environmental context for protecting national heritage lands and waters. If it is true that we are reaching an era with environmental tipping points, it is hard to imagine a more important time to prepare the next generation for avoiding perils and seizing opportunities than now. The history of the National Park System is encouraging because it is replete with the positive impacts of single individuals (both private citizens and agency personnel), as well as all levels of nongovernment organizations. The lesson is that everyone can make a difference in this arena.

As we write, it is difficult to imagine a time with a more divided public and so little that is universally agreed upon. Perhaps national heritage—expressed in the American covenant—can become a stronger focus of common interest and a rallying point for national cohesion. Some may remember that national parks were invoked as sites for "unity, hope, and healing" by Fran Mainella (NPS director, 2001–6) after 9/11.

As mentioned earlier, some modern perils are "something new under the sun." So tomorrow's challenges will likely be far beyond those faced by past generations of leaders. The increasing scale of the human endeavor and its inevitable impact on nature in the twenty-first century will pose pervasive dangers that will require our most informed, inspired, and unified effort as a people.

The environmental perils for modern generations are real. They are related to the statistics of human success, which are remarkable and well known. In 1820 the world's population was 1 billion, in 1900, 1.6 billion, and in 2000, 6.0 billion. At present (2019), the earth's human population is approximately 7.5 billion. The twentieth century (0.00025 of human history) hosted roughly 20 percent of all human years.[2]

On top of this explosion of humans' mere numerical presence, world economic activity has grown 120-fold since 1500. Notwithstanding gross inequities in distribution, we have nine times more per capita income on average than our ancestors had in 1500.[3] It is also alarming that the world park movement may become pressured to consider extraction of protected areas' resources as a tool for addressing world poverty. These strategic population and wealth-distribution issues cannot be solved by conservationists alone. These social issues require more systemic and long-term solutions that do not threaten the biosphere that supports the human species and 8–10 million others.

These world trends drive the environmental perils of our age and signal closing windows of opportunity for fully protecting the world's natural heritage overall—as well as that of each sovereign nation. And it rightfully falls on the United States to take a leadership role in championing its "best idea" successfully in this difficult future. This new age of perils will demand the most audacious and agile leadership the American public and the National Park Service have yet seen.

One Example of Global-Scale Peril: Climate Change

Global climate change is the universal threat whose impact will be felt far beyond the boundaries of any protected area. Yet it is important to consider how our national parks will fare as an American covenant and what can be done to protect parks when basic earth processes become significantly altered through human activity.

It's certain that weather patterns and events have begun to change and will continue to change dramatically in the future. For example, enhanced rates of sea level rise will certainly impact the Everglades severely and change the coastlines of many other coastal parks. Rates of coastal erosion will increase, and natural and cultural near-shore features will be inundated.

Cape Cod National Seashore has been key in bringing sea level rise to the park service's attention. In 1977 Cape Cod National Seashore found it necessary to move the historic (1897) Old Harbor Life

Saving Station due to coastal erosion. Awareness of the need to accommodate the dynamics of coastal shorelines accelerated in 1978 when the Seashore's Coast Guard Beach facilities were washed away (along with the Outer Most House of Henry Beston fame) due to a fierce nor'easter aided by sea level rise. Similarly, the NPS struggled but successfully moved the historic Bodie Island lighthouse at Cape Hatteras National Seashore, a project that began in the 1980s and was completed in 1999.

As the climate warms, species will extend their ranges north and, in some cases, to higher elevations. Some species will prosper, and others will fade. Some will invade new territory as it becomes hospitable. Diseases and plant and animal pests may move, wax, and wane as well. Regional climate projection models are still rudimentary but they suggest that rainfall and snowfall patterns will be different, with some regions getting much wetter and some drier. It appears likely that the west may become much drier, exhausting already oversubscribed water supplies. (Nevertheless, some cities are still encouraging growth and expecting that water will be found to support it.)

Catastrophic events are thought to be likely to increase in frequency and severity. What were rates of natural change will be augmented by this human-induced source of change, considered by most scientists to be significantly higher than the rates of climate change found in the historic trends recorded in glacial and sedimentary records. Patrick Gonzalez's projections of climate change in parks will, we believe, be confirmed.

Ecological, Social, and Political Implications

The recent trends in public understanding of climate change and the human role in accelerating it are encouraging. Many people accept the consensus of the world's scientists, but others need to see it firsthand, and some may always suspect a form of conspiracy against their real and imagined interests. Still others will not be convinced as long as there are really cold winters, errors are found in the global models as scientists slowly improve them, and distrust of government—and perhaps of science in general—grows. Nevertheless, climate change remains an unfortunate as well as an inconvenient truth.

Others are seeing climate change for themselves in the earlier return of robins each spring, the appearance of more southerly species moving north, and other signs of an earlier onset of spring in the northeast. For many, the dramatic photographs of the loss of summer Arctic ice or the disappearance of permafrost in Alaska will be convincing. At this time there seems to be enough distrust and disinformation to delay any unified and vigorous approach to addressing the root causes. Hence, education must be accurate, fast-tracked, and effective. National parks can play a much stronger role in this effort. Nevertheless, there are many reasons to plan now for action to reduce the risk of further disruption of the only viable habitat for humanity that we know of.

National parks will be subject to a changing climate as much as unprotected lands are. At the very least, climate change will be a test of the resilience of each ecosystem. Each species in the complex community to which they are adapted will encounter relatively rapid climatic change and adapt, move, or die out. However, if park lands are well understood and well managed for a high level of ecological integrity and resilience, they will be refugia for many species, suffer the least negative impact, and serve as reservoirs of intact natural systems. That is perhaps the best we can hope for but still an invaluable contribution to society. National parks will be as familiar remnants of nature as we will have. They will play a role not unlike that played by urban parks for many city dwellers today.

Park staffs may see impacts on the primary species their parks are known for; in those cases in which the surrounding lands are federal lands, collaborative orchestration of federal management regimes can be used to provide safe harbor for those species that move beyond the parks' boundaries. That is, if the political leadership so decides. Private landowners may be increasingly willing to help when our society begins to realize the high stakes of the atmospheric changes already being experienced and the need to work together.

As climate change wreaks havoc on water cycles, agricultural success, and the rate, intensity, and volatility of catastrophic events, there may be significant societal upheaval that will play out in new and unknown political processes. Therein lies perhaps the greatest threat to the stability of the American covenant: loss of the political will and stability to maintain national parks through all magnitudes of societal change.

On a smaller and less dramatic scale, political uncertainty is a peril that potentially challenges the National Park System with every election, especially with changes in presidential administrations. Following are examples based on Mike and Gary's firsthand observations of the changes in political winds that often distract management, shift the focus in the NPS, and thwart a consistent approach to the important work at hand.

A Recent Political History, of Sorts

At the beginning of our careers, the nation's environmental agenda had just prospered with the establishment of Earth Day and the support of President Richard Nixon for major environmental legislation. It had moved forward under President Jimmy Carter with the major achievement of the Alaska National Interest Lands Conservation Act. The pendulum of environmental momentum was then swung toward the expedited consumption of natural resources on public lands by the Reagan administration. Indeed, President

Reagan's controversial secretary of the Interior James Watt was widely reported to be certain that human domination of the earth was the proper order of things and it was best to get on with it. This view stemmed in some measure from a misquotation of Watt as saying, "God gave us these things to use. After the last tree is felled, Christ will come back."[4] Along with Watt came colorful assistant secretaries in the Department of the Interior who never saw an environmental issue or a species that couldn't benefit from hunting, fishing, grazing, extracting, or paving. Many NPS employees became legends for their defensive prowess in fighting a daily battle to keep national parks and their resources intact and provide rationales that fended off the use-it-up-now agenda. The NPS perked along positively and quietly under George H. W. Bush, who seemed to understand government well and also the need for careful approaches to managing public lands.

What happened next was interesting. Even professed environmentally friendly administrations can make holding course with the spirit of the parks' covenant difficult. The Clinton era, for example, was one of great enthusiasm for the potential of government—an enthusiasm not fully shared at the time by Congress. The Clinton administration was fond of proclaiming new administration initiatives almost weekly, always with a catchy name and a worthy goal. New ideas appeared at the National Park Service doorstep nearly every week—always worth pursuing, but always accompanied by no interest or funding from Congress. At the same time, Vice President Al Gore was enthusiastically asking government to do more with less and awarding symbolic hammers to those programs that achieved significant results. Gary's NPS social science program received one.

While new ideas and programs were fashionable in the Clinton administration, the administration also found it fashionable, and popular with Congress, to downsize the staff needed to implement them. One early downsizing effort offered a $25,000 bonus to employees willing to leave government service. In a few cases (in other agencies), whole field outposts were deserted, as legend has it, leaving the phones to just ring unattended. More often the most talented employees reappeared as consultants, and at much steeper pay scales, to do the same work they'd done under their agency.

Clinton's secretary of the Interior, Bruce Babbitt, was a great fan of science with a genuine love for parks. Secretary Babbitt became fascinated with advice from well-meaning but naive biologists in the U.S. Fish and Wildlife Service (FWS) who dreamed of resurrecting the National Biological Survey (NBS)—a romantic idea (for biologists) that had been unsuccessful in the 1930s. Babbitt began by taking all researchers from the U.S. Fish and Wildlife Service, the National Park Service, and the Bureau of Land Management and announcing that they would make up the new National Biological Survey. Therein the scientists would be independent of agency control or any chance of bias affecting research results. This change was presented as a *fait accompli* to everyone, including Congress.

There is a belief in political Washington that if one is to achieve anything substantial while in office, it is essential to act quickly in one's term of office in order to minimize the chance for opposition to form. The equally important adage, apparently less well known, is "Be sure that you don't surprise those who hold the purse-strings." Hence, one important source of opposition to the new bureau, Congress, quickly pushed back.

Meanwhile, the NBS concept of better, more centralized, independent, and effective government biological science was feared by some who thought it was a government conspiracy to seek out ("survey") endangered species on private lands in order to expand federal control of private lands—and thereby compromise private property rights. To quiet the controversy over the "national survey" issue, the National Biological Survey quickly renamed itself the National Biological

Service. Nevertheless, the first NBS budget request for a 28 percent increase was instead treated by Congress to a 20 percent overall cut. In the Everglades, even though the former NPS research scientists (Mike included) were assigned to the former FWS Science Center in Gainesville for administrative support, little support was forthcoming. Calls to the now-NBS Center's administrative officer asking for vehicles to tow research airboats into the Everglades first brought brave, optimistic projections that were soon replaced by sobbing. National Biological Service researchers were on their own. In what was becoming a tumultuous rout of the NBS, serious science, especially in parks, was taking a long recess.

Eventually the administration and the NBS ran for cover. The NBS was nestled under the protective wing of the U.S. Geological Survey, an agency not known for irritating Congress or anyone in any way. The National Biological Service became the *Biological* Research Division, interestingly, of the U.S. *Geological* Survey. Shortly thereafter, the first director of the National Biological Service, Ron Pulliam, a respected ecologist, resigned and returned to the University of Georgia. Professor Pulliam had optimistically brought his large fungus research collection with him to Washington to continue his studies in his spare time. Instead he received an intense postgraduate education on "Contract with America" politics.[5] The Biological Research Division remains in the U.S. Geological Survey today, in a state of perpetual reorganization, and there are currently fewer research scientists stationed long-term in national parks than in the 1980s. While well-intentioned, divorcing park researchers from park management reversed for a time the slow progress NPS had been making to build science into park operations in a meaningful way.

The National Park Service itself was reorganized and downsized ("reinvented") according to the "latest innovative management concept." Flattened organizations meant fewer, smaller central offices. Resources were put in the field, "where the action was." But other costs were incurred because centralization of services in regional offices had been allowing for smaller park staffs. The number of regional offices was shrunk from ten to seven, but pressure from powerful congressmen kept the Seattle and Boston offices open (with skeletal staffing) nevertheless. The ten regional directors became seven field directors (who were informally derided as "field marshals"). With the decentralization came poorer program evaluation and a greater lack of supervision and accountability.

Years later, the flattened organization quietly and unofficially, and not unlike cells reaggregating in a petri dish, resumed its old organizational structure, except that its central offices remained cannibalized and without the means to effectively provide technical services, let alone adequate supervision or accountability, for the hundreds of superintendents who were now directly managed by seven downsized regional offices. The Clinton administration left disappointed in NPS for its general intransigence and notably for the failure of its management to provide sufficiently severe punishment to its employees when the NPS-prescribed fire program at Bandolier National Park in New Mexico accidently burned much of the town of Los Alamos. Years of tinkering had left the park service off-balance and in general disarray. And it was not prepared for what was to come next.

Next was the George W. Bush administration and Interior Secretary Gale Norton. Norton had previously been attorney general in Colorado and was a protégé of James Watt. She and her politically appointed Interior leadership felt that the pendulum of prioritizing resource protection in parks over resource use had swung too far toward resource protection.

Secretary Norton, on her first day in office, delivered her point of view to Department of the Interior employees: stringent environmental restraint is misguided and bad for the economy. Government, not people, is the problem. Environmental regulations must require only voluntarily adherence; they should be rare and be baited with incentives. She wasn't entirely wrong about federal regulations, of course. They can be overblown and sometimes inadvertently or unnecessarily crippling, yet our environmental laws are responsible for much of our current quality of life (many but not all of us have good air to breathe—and can actually see down into the Grand Canyon—can drink and swim in clean water, and more). This was a time of challenge to hold on to those reasonable environmental regulations that are fair and are worthy of respect and enforcement.

In her first presentation to department employees (Mike was there) the secretary thus made it known that people were not to be treated as causing problems environmentally and that government, most especially the federal government, needed to get out of their way. In essence, parks should stop saying no to people so often. The careful NPS dance of human use within necessary limits was disdained in favor of reverence for the needs and wants of stakeholders. The main Interior building became a favorite stopover for a flood of interest groups with their own perspectives as to what national parks could provide for them, now. Those westerners with their minds on grazing, hunting in parks, and ridding themselves of federal laws were feeling their oats, and a sea of cowboy hats ebbed and flowed daily down the halls of main Interior. Moreover, the political appointees—those in leadership positions appointed anew by the White House after every presidential election—were an interesting mix of libertarians, creationists, and sagebrush rebels—all with differing brands of distrust for the federal government.

Obviously there are great uncertainties in managing for the long term in a system with such frequent swings and upheavals in leadership. Here we offer an example that illustrates the high stakes involved for the nation's heritage—and the American covenant reflected in national parks—by swings in the political pendulum.

The Priority Date of Water

In the west, the availability of water and the complex process to assign the rights to use it underpins the precarious but continuing development of western cities and irrigation-dependent agriculture. Water supply and irrigation projects can have huge environmental consequences (as we have seen as well in South Florida). Suffice it to say that water allocations already oversubscribe water availability in many systems, and the impact on nature is far less understood or carefully considered than people realize. Anxious to get stakeholders a better seat at the table, Secretary Norton's legal counsel quickly moved to approach federal water rights in national parks from more of a perspective of state water users—with potentially devastating implications.

Many parks in the west (and again, Everglades is an eastern example) are threatened by rapacious urban and agricultural development up to and beyond the limits of the water available. Thus it is absolutely necessary to ensure that national parks retain their federal water rights at the level of the water necessary to fulfill the long-term mission described in the enabling legislation for each park. Over decades, the National Park Service had been moving to identify, quantify, and thus protect the water rights of the national parks in western states under the federal reserved water rights doctrine. That basically means that when reserving federal lands the federal government retains the right to the amount of water necessary to meet the purpose for which those lands are being set aside. The date of the reservation (the "priority date") of said water is all-important, placing it above any subsequent claims for water. Establishing and quantifying a claim takes place in the state court system and is extremely complicated, arcane, and difficult.

An instructive example of high-stakes peril to the national parks is the water rights court case filed by environmental groups in 2003 to protect Black Canyon of the Gunnison National Park in Colorado. At the end of the Clinton administration, a long process had resulted in the NPS's filing an application to quantify the water rights of Black Canyon. The canyon, located in west-central Colorado, was originally protected as a national monument by Herbert Hoover in 1933, "for the preservation of the spectacular gorges and additional features of scenic, scientific, and educational interest."[6] The monument was converted to a national park by the Black Canyon Act of 1999 (P.L. 106-76). The quantity of water necessary for protection of the park's spectacular gorge includes a certain base flow in the river *plus* occasional peak flows—"the great spring tidal flashes of the river" cited in the park's enabling legislation. Reservation of this water for the park would have a priority date of 1933, preempting any later claims for unappropriated water.

National Park Service technical staff had determined the minimum needs for base flows in the river as well as that needed for the occasional peak flows. In 1978 the Colorado State Court awarded an unquantified water right to the park with a priority date beginning in 1933 and with an instruction to file a final and specific quantification of the amount of water necessary to fulfill the park's purposes. This quantification filing, three days before the end of the Clinton administration, quickly attracted the attention of Norton's Coloradan political appointees. The NPS filing, with its carefully reasoned technical underpinnings, soon became the object of a more "innovative" approach by the Department of the Interior that would meet the needs of the many other stakeholders—including Interior's Bureau of Reclamation and its agricultural constituents, as well as the Department of Energy's Western Area Power Administration. These agencies control upstream Colorado River water flows and market the hydroelectric power created by water releases through the complex of dams begun in 1956.

This "innovative" approach was developed by Secretary Norton's counselor and deputy solicitor. His approach was to first curtly dismiss the NPS career water rights experts from the process and then to unilaterally enter into agreements with the state of Colorado's Water Conservation Board. The resulting agreement guaranteed the park a base flow of three hundred cubic feet per second with a 1933 priority date, but relinquished the 1933 priority date for any peak flows. With the Colorado Water Conservation Board in charge, the likelihood of an NPS priority date for the peak flows would be slim to none. The flashes of high water that created and maintained Black Canyon were being given away and lost forever.

The Department of the Interior's reasoning was later laid out in responses to a suit filed by seven environmental watchdog organizations against Secretary Norton and NPS director Mainella (both political appointees). The department's rationale was that the agreement, entered into without any public involvement process (as required under the National Environmental Policy Act), was "a creative solution to meeting multiple needs."[7] Such reasoning perplexed the United States District Court for the District of Colorado.

In its opinion the court recognized that the agreements entered into by the federal defendants and the state of Colorado "bring a sense of relief to a number of users of the river because the agreements eliminate uncertainty created by competition for a crucial water supply." But the court continued, "In their zeal to reach a solution to the competing interests, however, the Defendants ignore the right of the public to be involved in such a major and significant decision." And further, "A decision to enter into agreements which permanently give up a priority to a resource which must be 'saved for all generations' must be made in public view and not behind closed doors 'with the public's interest in mind.'"[8]

The court found that the effect of the secretary's counsel's agreements with the state "was actually to remove the administration of the

Black Canyon resources from the National Park Service in direct contravention of the National Park Service Organic Act, the Black Canyon Act and the Wilderness Act" (p. 30). Finally, the court stated that it "accordingly finds that it was arbitrary, capricious and an abuse of discretion to enter into the agreements and relinquish a 1933 priority to the full quantity of water necessary for the preservation of the Black Canyon. Such a relinquishment is nonsensical" (p. 31). The matter was "remanded to the National Park Service for further proceedings consistent with this decision." Interior's legal counsel (David Bernhardt, who became President Trump's second secretary of the Interior) was thus forced to allow NPS water rights professionals to reengage in a difficult water allocation process. The stakes are incredibly high in such cases, as insuring adequate protection for the conditions that created Black Canyon of the Gunnison is fundamental to maintaining this national park unimpaired.

This example—a close call—illustrates the vulnerability of national park resources and the American covenant to political interests and agendas. It is just one of many assaults on the integrity of national parks that occur year after year—in this case with a happy ending. To keep the covenant, park resources must win every time, or somehow be shielded in the first place from constant pressure from vested interests.

Attempted Tinkerings

Perhaps the use-it-up-now aspiration of the Norton era reached its zenith in a curious saga in which the Assistant Secretary for Fish, Wildlife, and Parks (a high-level political appointee) tried to unilaterally rewrite the National Park Service's official Management Policies. Cited earlier, these policies are expressed in the precisely worded guidebook for managing and protecting national parks. These policies have evolved and been improved over the decades. Each word has been carefully chosen, argued over, applied, and reworked over the years to assist every park superintendent in navigating sensibly, consistently, and fairly almost any situation. They contain the basis for saying "no" when he or she has to protect resources but give enough latitude for a wise park manager to be flexible if warranted.

This assistant secretary, a personable former Chamber of Commerce official in Cody, Wyoming, with apparent ties to the White House, wished to open up parks to new uses and remove old restrictions that were not "people friendly." In his new version, managing with the goal of "avoiding unacceptable impacts" was changed to "managing only for avoiding impairment of National Parks." The career NPS employees quickly interpreted this new policy as their being told to manage park resources for conditions "just this side of dead." Such changes, while seemingly "just common sense," represented a real likelihood of "wear and tear" and gradual decline in the health of park resources and a spiral of decline in the quality of national park visits over time.

The attempt to soften the Management Policies was a reflection of great sympathy for unfettered enjoyment for today's visitors, especially those represented by the motorized recreational vehicle lobby. Dirt bikers, snowmobilers, personal watercraft advocates, mountain bikers, and others are often not satisfied with National Park access, which is usually more restricted than on Bureau of Land Management, National Forest, or National Wildlife Refuge lands, as well as in state, regional, and county parks.

Segments of the recreation industry had for years pressured national parks for greater access for the widest range of recreational activities. During Roger Kennedy's stint as director under President Clinton, a hostile congressional hearing was held to bring pressure on him to open up parks to motorized and other industry-favored activities in national parks. There was great tension in the hearing room when the erudite Kennedy was asked the first question: Can you tell us how the National Park Service views recreation in national parks? Kennedy pronounced, in a stentorian voice: "Recreation in national parks is informed delight, not feckless merriment." It was apparent that the chairman was baffled by this answer (wondering "Are we for or against feckless merriment? Where do snowmobiles fit in?"). Amid some consternation and whispering among members and staff, the hearing was soon adjourned and not resumed during Kennedy's tenure.

Secretary Norton's new, massively changed version of the NPS Management Policies for parks was soon out in the public view. Much to the department's surprise, a firestorm of public and nationwide press outcry (over a hundred editorials against), as well as serious rebellion within the NPS career ranks, eventually turned back the effort. The author of their new laissez-faire version of the Management Policies was eventually banished to the department's "competitive sourcing" office, where he would then oversee the contracting out of Interior (and National Park Service) jobs to private firms.

After six years, Secretary Norton exited to become senior counsel for a major oil company. Her deputy, previously a champion of mountaintop removal strip-mining, went to jail as a result of the Abramoff scandal, and her staff's interference with DOI science and the implementation of the Endangered Species Act remained under investigation for some time.

Swings of Fortune

With the election of Barack Obama in 2008, the fortunes of the NPS and, broadly, federal conservation writ large improved dramatically. For the first time the directors of the NPS, USFWS, and BLM, as well as the chief of the U.S. Forest Service, were all selected from within the agency's professional leadership. Director Jarvis had a science degree and a long career as a resource biologist, superintendent of several parks, and regional director. He had helped lead the effective pushback against the weakened and flawed draft changes in the NPS Management Policies. Symbolically and strategically, one of his first hires was the first-ever science adviser to the director (Gary). This new position—which did not oversee science activities of the NPS but provided direct scientific advice to the director—signaled a needed reemphasis of science in the parks.

The appointment was quickly followed by a ramping up of an ambitious NPS Climate Change Program, the establishment of yet another high-level Science Committee of the NP System Advisory Board, increases in the NPS science budget and the number of scientific personnel for climate change science, and the development of an official science integrity policy and code of conduct.

Using an approach they labeled "strategic intention," Jarvis and Gary (along with new regional and associate directors appointed by Jarvis) took advantage of the NPS's centennial year (2016) and proactively advanced the NPS mission—creating an innovative program to attract new park visitors and advocates, completing long-awaited resource management projects (such as the final removal of Elwha Dam in Washington State's Olympic National Park), and adding twenty-six new parks, including Katahdin Woods and Waters National Monuments in Maine, Castle Mountains National Monument in California, and others. These advances ended abruptly with the election of Donald Trump.

In the first years of the new administration, two national monuments were dramatically reduced in size to allow for mining and gas development. Regulations to protect NPS lands were weakened or withdrawn, off-road vehicle use was permitted in several vulnerable parks, protections of migratory birds and wildlife were reduced, climate change science was suppressed, the requirement that superintendents have a minimal scientific literacy was undone, and the NPS was reorganized to weaken its focus on upholding the Organic Act and to politicize the professional leadership.[9] The full inventory of challenges to the

NPS and conservation across the nation posed by the Trump administration is yet to be compiled, but it is very clear that partisan policies and the pendulum of power are currently at odds with the NPS mission.

National parks need to be exempted from such harsh swings in political support if the American covenant is to remain unbroken. The drama and suspense of changing political perspectives are real and proximate forms of peril that national parks face. The degree of future peril will be determined by whether citizens become more aware of, thankful for, and caring about their environment—and act to ensure that national parks are largely exempt from political vagaries—or whether they continue to demand more and more from the earth and eventually decide to let the wealthy and well-connected loot what's left in the last treasure troves: their national parks.

Other Perils

There are also other sources of modern peril. Perhaps the most insidious—and unwarranted—is the "post-modernist" undermining of the concept of nature itself and the value of "natural" areas and "wilderness" as mentioned in chapter 5. There is a trend in some academic spheres—and some board rooms of big conservation organizations that see alliances with the corporate world as the salvation of the conservation movement—to deny that true nature still exists.

The argument of those with this view is something like this: protected natural areas, and especially wilderness areas, are ephemera—human intellectual constructs invoking a pristine nature that does not exist.[10] They reason that since humans have roamed the earth and in some way changed nature everywhere, pristine nature, unadulterated by humans, is an illusion; hence, preservation "game over." If that view is a given, why not actively maximize the management of nature for direct human benefit—again, seeing the earth as one big garden?

One can easily see the appeal of this perspective to those interested in cashing in on nature's remaining treasure troves.

An ancillary, if circular, argument is that since humans are part of nature, anything they do is "natural"; therefore, anything that benefits humans benefits nature. (Roger Kennedy once asked: "If humans are a part of nature, if I shoot you, do you die of natural causes?") Nevertheless, the argument is that it's time to stop trying to fight the losing battle of keeping human intervention off limits and to start seriously gardening the earth for the maximum benefit of humankind.

In the face of perilous environmental trends, rejection of the traditional principles of conservation has some appeal, and it certainly avoids a lot of conflict and disappointment. This sophistry has become very fashionable in some circles. While the intellectual exercise can be fascinating to some, it can also be valuable to those who would profit from access to the last and best natural treasures still extant. For us it is an ignominious route to failing to live up to the terms and ideals of the American covenant.

This kind of thinking should be very foreign to anyone who is familiar with the daily work in national parks. The National Park System includes 44 million acres of wilderness in forty-seven national parks. It is irrelevant whether humans have trod there before, set fires, or hunted mammoths. These are simply places where there are no permanent human populations or structures and nature prevails. Humans are welcome, but human technology and its impacts are tightly controlled, roughly equivalent to the level of impact of an early humanoid without hunting privileges. And when you visit any wilderness area you will know the difference between them and areas where humans dominate. This seems simple enough, but somehow it is not.

It should also be very easy for all to understand the value of the work the NPS does in all the sites it manages that are not wilderness. As we have seen, many of the national park units that find their way into the

NPS are heavily impacted and some are quite nature-impaired. The unchanging goal for park management and staff working under the NPS Management Policies is to minimize human impacts wherever possible, even if the goal of eliminating all unacceptable impacts is not achievable. Over time, the intent and the result is to gradually restore them insofar as possible and practical. So many national park sites are increasingly better off environmentally (with the exception, of course, of the mounting global-scale issues); it is academic whether they are pristine nature or not. A visit to Padre Island National Seashore in Texas (a former flattened, denuded cattle ranch) or Rock Creek Park in Washington, D.C. (once cleared farmland), will be convincing. Parks are places (or, more theatrically, stages) where nature plays out as unimpaired as possible. It is hard to argue against that policy as being the more worthy of and beneficial to the long-term health of the planet than attempting to maximize the short-term benefits for just the human species among all others.

The ongoing, intense pressure from state fish and game agencies and hunting lobbyists for access to hunting in parks is both shortsighted and disruptive to the role of parks as refuges where evolution can play out unimpeded. Yet, as hunting continues to be less popular, somehow the intensity of the pressure to allow it in national parks seems to gain momentum.

Political pressure to allow fishing has been even more intense and devastating in marine parks. Because of the protection they ostensibly provide (as reservoirs of resources vanishing elsewhere), national parks would seem to be the best places to find fish—and hence enjoy good fishing for sport. Marine parks might have been so once. A study of Virgin Islands National Park waters found that there were more fish outside the park boundary than inside.[11] The traditional fishing practices of local islanders have been replaced by modern gear, including increased motorized access by both locals and visitors. Intense recreational fishing adds to the pressure on fish stocks, with rates of removal surpassing reproductive potential. Similarly, at Biscayne National Park in Florida, where jurisdiction over fishing has been ceded to the Florida Fish and Wildlife Conservation Commission, researchers at the University of Miami found that it took many dives to spot the first grouper, a fish historically plentiful in these waters. Biscayne National Park has recently struggled mightily to turn this situation around with a new fishery management plan—with little real progress to date.[12]

Allowing fishing—essentially aquatic hunting—in national parks is a strong tradition that goes back to the earliest parks and the quest to provide visitor entertainment. This leaves important elements of national parks curiously unprotected. In the current political arena, the National Park Service cannot withstand the pressure sure to follow any proposed change in fishing policy. Nevertheless, protection of all elements of wild life in parks—especially top predators—is vitally important. Protected fish populations within park boundaries would in many cases replenish upstream and downstream habitats (or adjacent or downcurrent marine habitats). This could guarantee "fishing forever"— the stated goal of commercial and recreational fishing lobbyists who nevertheless pursue the tradition of fishing everywhere, now.

Fishing lobbies often fiercely defend their "right" to catch the last few fish rather than admit that the old rules and traditions won't work anymore. The freedom to fish—often, perhaps rightfully, portrayed as one of our finer family traditions and individual freedoms—is a powerful notion. That is, until the fish are gone. The history of fishing in the United States and elsewhere is one of serial depletion of fishing stocks that would still be abundant today if managed wisely. It is especially sad that our coastal national parks and seashores have remained largely unprotected. Implementation (or even the mention of) establishing "no-take zones" is often hotly opposed, and its pursuit requires great courage. A vision of what might again be the bounty that once was may eventually increase public support for a science-based array of no-fishing zones—many in parks—that will underpin the ability for us all to fish forever. This can still be done.

As noted earlier, the American covenant that is a national park is codified in the Organic Act, interpreted in the NPS Management Policies and tailored to each park by its enabling legislation. These would seem to provide ample protection. But not necessarily. There is probably no better recent example of how this approach can fail than the recent legislation affecting Acadia National Park. Acadia NP was established for the area's protection and enjoyment and its scientific value. Yet recent appeals from local commercial clammers and "wormers" (sellers of seaworms for bait) garnered popular support locally and with the entire Maine congressional delegation to amend Acadia National Park's hundred-year-old protective legislation to remove management authority from its intertidal lands. This was achieved by adding a brief section into the Acadia National Park Boundary Clarification Act of 2019.

This diminishment of park authority in favor of commercial harvesting of important elements of the intertidal food chain saw no pushback from park advocacy groups or from the NPS. Lack of concern was justified by the many fervent supporters of the park (who just went all out in celebrating the park's centennial) who saw such harvesting as a "traditional use." Seeing clammers "working the mud" on the intertidal flats is comforting and picturesque to some, to the extent that the protective role of the national park as refuge and laboratory didn't matter. To others the weakening of Acadia's original legislation symbolized a victory for the "little guy" against the federal government. Acadia NP staff had been lax in consistently implementing NPS policies against commercial harvesting of resources, adding to the clammers' justification of "traditional use." So it was surprisingly easy and locally uncontroversial to set this precedent of giving away, for sale, park resources to a "deserving" constituency of harvesters. In our view, this loss of control over its intertidal resources violates the intent of the hundred-year-old protective covenant for Acadia NP and compromises the constant and often hard-fought on-going struggles to keep commercial fishing (and myriad other "traditional uses") out of national parks. Clam harvesters have recently claimed that driving their pickup trucks to where the clams are taken is also part of their tradition.

These are some foreseeable sources of peril. Should new generations decide to tackle the issue of human domination, isolate parks from the vexing concern of political exploitation, and avoid the dangers of intellectual sophistry, the future could offer grand and happy possibilities. While the issues discussed above seem daunting, there remain satisfying opportunities to enhance the American covenant by seizing the substantial opportunities that exist in the American landscape even in the midst of peril.

Opportunities

An example of the National Park Service's leadership and tenacity in pursuit of improving the future landscape is seen on the Elwha River in Olympic National Park. Hundreds of thousands of salmon (of ten species) once migrated up the Elwha to spawn—until early in the 1900s. Then two dams were built that blocked salmon from 90 percent of the river, reducing the salmon run to around three thousand fish. Now, following the dictates of National Park Service law and policy, Olympic National Park has orchestrated the world's largest dam removal project and one of the world's largest river restoration projects. The opportunity to restore the salmon run promises far-reaching positive impacts with the renewed transfer of nutrients from the ocean up the river for both wildlife and human consumption. Momentum for removal of the Elwha and Glines dams surged with the Elwha River Ecosystem and Fisheries Restoration Act of 1992. After many years of research and working with partners and stakeholders, including the City of Port Angeles and the Lower Elwha Klallam Tribe, dam removal began in 2011 and was completed by 2014. It will take a while for the hydrology, sediments, and nutrients to equilibrate and salmon populations and the species that depend on them to fully recover, but the salmon are returning. The success of these projects provides a joyous prospect—especially for the Klallam people—of seeing nature recover. The Elwha restoration is a case study in seizing opportunities and is certainly illustrative of why parks matter.

Opportunities are, of course, a matter of priorities. Overall, Congress has viewed the NPS budget as nonessential. The only justification for that position is that the national parks are established on purely political whims rather than as part of a serious scientific approach to achieving a representative system of national heritage and ecological reserves. Therein lies an opportunity to reform the process by which national parks are created.

We have seen glimpses of the closing window of opportunities for the creation of large natural parks evidenced in the developmental history of our National Park System. The trend is toward fewer, smaller, more ecologically and politically compromised additions to the system, reflecting both a lack of political will and a landscape that has increasingly been claimed for development. Congress has been happy to add sites favored locally without an overall strategy yet has been ambivalent about providing funding levels that cover the operational costs of the growing system, whose units are now predominantly cultural and historic sites.

The Second Century Commission, hosted by the National Parks Conservation Association in preparation for the NPS Centennial in 2016, recommended the development of a science-based plan for a representative national park system as a goal for the centennial. There was also some concern as to who should carry out this analysis. Since the National Park Service has become very shy about the subject of new areas following considerable pressure and restrictions applied by an of-ten hostile Congress, the commission's blue-ribbon panel (which in-cluded Justice Sandra Day O'Connor, Senators Howard Baker and Bennett Johnston, Governor Tony Knowles of Alaska, Rita Colwell, former director of the National Science Foundation under President Clinton, and other leaders from a wide array of backgrounds) recom-mended that the National Academy of Sciences (or a presidential com-mission) be the source of the science-based plan.[13] This has not occurred.

The next in a long, successive line of reports on NPS science was the NP System Advisory Board's *Revisiting Leopold: Resource Steward-ship in the National Parks,* whose writing was led by Gary and Rita Colwell. The Science Committee of the board and its report recom-mended elevating the role of science in NPS decision making, ex-panding the inventory and monitoring of park resources, establishing a minimum level of science literacy for superintendents, and expand-ing the cadre of NPS scientists and stationing them in parks. The re-port also restated the need for full representation of American landscapes (and seascapes) within the National Park System.

For us, the value of a strategically designed National Park System ranks up there with the priorities given to national defense as well as those given to the public and economic health of the nation. There may be a great opportunity to raise awareness of the link between a nation's environmental health and national identity and its long-term national defense. If the funding priorities of Congress were tractable—somehow breaking the hold of the military-industrial complex—the trend that we now see of the military responding to natural catastrophes and hu-manitarian interventions might well extend to defense of the national heritage. There is great opportunity here, as the purchase price of one B-2 bomber ($2.4 billion) is nearly the same as the annual budget of the NPS. There is a similar connection to be made with national public health and education priorities if national parks can play a stronger role in teaching the American public to appreciate active, environmentally sound lifestyles, science, and prudent economic development.

While Secretary of the Interior Babbitt served under President Clinton, he kept a scorecard of the Clinton administration's land conservation achievements versus those of Teddy Roosevelt. Clinton was challenged to seize similar conservation opportunities and by the end of his second administration, according to Babbitt's tally, they were successful. President George W. Bush is credited with the establishment of one of the largest protected areas on the planet, the Papahānaumokuākea Marine National Monument, in Hawaiian waters, at the end of his administration. The Obama administration acted in 2016 to expand this monument by a factor of four to make it the biggest in the world.

President Obama also established Bears Ears National Monument in southeastern Utah, protecting 1,351,849 acres under Bureau of Land Management jurisdiction, containing invaluable Native American cultural resources and a unique landscape. President Trump, at the behest of the energy-development enthusiasts newly installed at the Department of the Interior, reduced the size of the monument by 85 percent, a decision being challenged in court.

With the covenant as a priority, every president can have an incredible impact on conservation, and competition among presidents as to their success in leaving a legacy of national heritage protection ought to be encouraged. Such a priority should be part of their campaign platforms and be a screening mechanism for voters. A sea change in national conservation politics is needed, and such change is possible.

An Inventory for the Future

In hopes that a new environmentally oriented administration would want to build a Teddy Roosevelt–scale legacy of national heritage protection, four leading ecological scientists wrote to President Obama's new secretary of the Interior, Ken Salazar, with their list of stellar areas that should be considered for national park status.[14] These scientists have spent their careers studying the natural diversity of the United States and were asked to participate in developing a vision of how the NPS could better manage migratory species. Traditionally the NPS has been very passive in its concern for migratory species that leave park boundaries. The approach has long been basically "Let's hope they return." A more collaborative and active partnership among all countries that "co-manage" migratory species across their life cycles is long overdue.

While urging more aggressive support for reducing the increasing barriers facing migratory species, these scientists developed a new set of potential areas whose designation would preserve some of the remaining underrepresented great natural ecosystems of the United States. Some of the areas they recommended are under federal ownership of some kind, so it would be a matter of changing agency jurisdiction or management paradigm—or proclaiming them as national monuments under the Antiquities Act. Transfer to the National Park System should be routine and noncontroversial whenever the combination of protection with public access is warranted. Other candidate areas would involve state and private lands, and in many such cases there would have to be a willing network of environmental, economic, and local citizen interest to support that effort. Here are twelve examples in the scientists' words:

1. The San Juan Mountains in southwestern Colorado and adjacent New Mexico are mostly National Forest lands at present, a spectacular wild mountain landscape and the site of the last confirmed grizzly bear south of the Greater Yellowstone ecosystem. Our recommendation includes the South San Juan Wilderness in Colorado, linked to the Cruces Basin Wilderness in New Mexico, and encompassing lower elevation areas

with piñon-juniper, ponderosa pine, Gambel oak, and other ecosystems poorly represented in the National Park System. Protecting a full and intact elevation gradient would provide opportunities for species to move upslope with climate change.

2. Kissimmee Prairies in south-central Florida—A mixture of state, private, and military (Avon Park Air Force Range) land at present, this area straddles the Kissimmee River, the headwaters of the Everglades. The outstanding ecosystem type within the area is the imperiled Florida dry prairie. This is an unusual, amazingly pristine, and striking landscape containing vast open grasslands, with the highest diversity of plants of any treeless grassland in North America, plus several endemic and rare animal species. It would be unlike any other area in the National Park System.

3. Oregon High Desert in southeastern Oregon—Many scenic sagebrush-dominated landscapes exist in the Oregon High Desert, but arguably the most biologically important and magnificent is the area from Hart Mountain National Wildlife (Antelope) Refuge, south-southwest to Sheldon National Wildlife Refuge (in Nevada, bordering Oregon), then northeast to the Catlow Rim, Malheur National Wildlife Refuge, Steens Mountain National Monument, and the Alvord Desert. Most of this area is already managed by the Department of the Interior (BLM and USFWS) with private inholdings. Little-known areas, such as the spectacular Lone Mountain with its rock pinnacles, natural bridges, and bighorn sheep population, are encompassed in this proposal.

4. Isla de Vieques—This glorious island is just offshore of Puerto Rico. Some of it is now protected within a National Wildlife Refuge. The island as a whole features pristine beaches, coastal lagoons, mangrove wetlands, sub-tropical dry forest, coral reefs, and seagrass beds, as well as priceless archeological and

historic features. The Caribbean Basin is one of the richest hotspots of biodiversity on Earth but is deficient in protected areas. This treasure is clearly of national park quality and would do much to redress this inadequacy.

5. Alaka'i Swamp on the island of Kauai in the Hawaiian Islands—This rugged and beautiful landscape (a montane wet forest, not a swamp) is famous for having perhaps the highest rainfall on earth (average 426 inches annually over the last century) and far more importantly, the highest concentration of endemic and endangered species anywhere in the United States. Clearly this is one of the premier conservation priorities in North America and the world, and it is not completely protected at present. Many of its endemic species are likely to vanish forever in the coming decades unless this extraordinary ecosystem is well protected and well managed.

6. Sky Islands—This stunning 70,000 sq. mile region of southeastern Arizona and southwestern New Mexico is globally outstanding because of its rich diversity of species and habitats, its history of ground-breaking biological studies (for example, by Forrest Shreve), and as the 'birthplace' of Aldo Leopold's land ethic. The Chiricahuas, Dragoons, Pinalenos, and Tumacacoris are among more than forty Sky islands (mountains within intervening valleys) that make up the region. Many of the species that occur here are found nowhere else in the United States.

7. East Montana grasslands—Large expanses of eastern Montana are sparsely populated and still cloaked in native grasslands. We focus on the area of Montana adjacent to Saskatchewan. This large, diverse region of mixed-grass prairie, with healthy populations of several imperiled grassland birds and charismatic wildlife species such as pronghorn—a species and family that is endemic to North America—presents an unparalleled

opportunity to protect an endangered ecosystem that straddles the U.S./Canada border.

8. Apalachicola Lowlands—This landscape, lying mostly on the eastern side of the Apalachicola River in the Florida panhandle, shows up in the maps produced by The Nature Conservancy and NatureServe as one of the three major hotspots of biodiversity east of the Mississippi River. The Apalachicola National Forest, the largest block of public land in this landscape, is known for having the highest total species diversity and largest number of endangered and threatened species of any U.S. National Forest. It includes the largest remaining area of contiguous longleaf pine forest (one of America's rarest and least-protected ecosystems) and the largest population of endangered red-cockaded woodpeckers on earth, as well as extraordinary bluffs and ravines along the Apalachicola River with many endemic species. This entire landscape would make an exceptional national park.

9. Klamath-Siskiyou Mountains—The rugged Klamath and Siskiyou Mountains of northwestern California and southwestern Oregon are famous as a hotspot of endemism, a refugium for ancient lineages of plants (including the highest diversity of conifer tree species north of central Mexico), and for their bizarre geology, including substantial areas of serpentine with Jeffrey pine forest and pitcher plant bogs. This region, which consists mainly of several national forests, is of international significance and clearly deserves national park status.

10. Roan Mountain—Renowned botanist Asa Gray described Roan Mountain as the most beautiful mountain east of the Rockies. An endemic species here, Gray's lily, is named for him. Less well-known than the Smoky Mountains, the Roan Mountain highlands of North Carolina and Tennessee contain

arguably the most spectacular scenery, including the most extensive array of grassy mountaintop "balds," in the Appalachian chain, along with one of the highest concentrations of rare and endemic species in the Southern Appalachians (which, as a region, is one of the biodiversity hotspots of North America). Consisting of national forest land, state parks, and some private land, this landscape, from the lowlands to the peaks, would be one of the finest national parks in the East.

11. Henry Mountains and Dirty Devil River—Located just west of Canyonlands National Park, this even more remote landscape would be an exceptional national park on its own or as an addition to the Canyonlands National Park. The Henry Mountains were the last mountain chain to be named—by John Wesley Powell in honor of Joseph Henry, the first secretary of the Smithsonian Institution—in the lower forty-eight states, which attests to their remoteness. Between them and the Canyonlands is a spectacular series of gorges of the Dirty Devil River and its tributaries, and nearby tributaries (such as Kickapoo Canyon) of the Colorado River. This new park would offer protection to one of the largest and most genetically pure herds of bison, which were introduced to the Henry Mountains in 1941, and sustain their migration.

12. Mobile-Tensaw Delta—Directly north of Alabama's Mobile Bay, this is a vast region of wetlands second only to the Mississippi Delta in size. This region is home to one of the most diverse assemblages of wild life in the entire United States. Along with the Tennessee River watershed, this is the primary hotspot of freshwater biodiversity in North America. America's freshwater species have been notably excluded from our National Park System, notwithstanding the alarming rate at which many groups (fishes, freshwater mussels, for example)

are declining or becoming endangered. The Mobile-Tensaw Delta is also historically rich and played a major role in the exploration and settlement of Alabama. The Deep South remains deficient in national parks, and this biologically significant area would fill a huge gap in the inventory.[15]

The recommendations of these ecologists did not extend to opportunities in the marine environment. Yet the current array of marine protected areas that safeguard our nation's marine heritage is sadly lacking in many ways. Even what has been achieved has been compromised severely. With the near-collapse of so many marine fisheries, there is an even more pressing need to seize opportunities to achieve a representative reflection of our nation's remarkable marine heritage within the National Park System.

There are indeed enormous opportunities to improve conditions in our oceans. While it is perfectly logical that the effects of greenhouse gas increases in our atmosphere spill over in every direction, it is hard to conceive that the seemingly limitless extent of the oceans does not protect them from harm. Nevertheless, long-term thermal and chemical changes (such as acidification) are being forced by increasing atmospheric CO_2 levels. Inexorably accruing at a global scale, these changes will be just as inexorably difficult to reverse.

Ocean acidification and thermal increases that may modify ocean currents are potential nightmares that elude an easy fix and are beyond any advantages that would accrue from a strategic approach to national park or protected-area designation. Nonetheless, the changing ocean can be best served by not piling on additional stresses such as overfishing and invasions of invasive species, plastics, and other pollutants. Seizing the opportunity to construct an effective network of truly protected areas would be the best this generation could offer now—and it would pay huge dividends.

The marine sphere presents perhaps the most wide-open opportunity to do the rewarding work necessary to sustain our rich heritage. For too long the oceans have been thought of as an inexhaustible last frontier that needed no protection. The U.S. National Marine Protected Area Center inventoried managed areas in U.S. waters and determined that even with 1,688 marine protected areas, at least 97 percent of U.S. territorial waters were still available for fishing in 2008.[16]

"Swim Like Hell"

Gary Davis, one of a very few NPS marine scientists, now retired, spent much of his career trying to stem the serial depletion of abalone species in the kelp forests of Channel Islands National Park in California and became the champion of the long-term monitoring of "park vital signs." Davis refers to the "tyranny of euphemisms" in the field of marine protection. Fish, shellfish, and other marine life are spoken of in terms of landings, metric tons, catch, and by-catch. But removing them from their complex communities is not much different from harvesting predators and prey on land. The impacts are just out of sight—and hence largely out of mind. Davis argues that some truth in advertising should be applied to the levels of protection provided by marine sanctuaries, wildlife refuges, and national parks. There is little sanctuary, or refuge, for commercially valuable marine species in all but a few recent "no-take" reserve designations.

Why is this important? Davis reflects that in his youth he worked on party fishing boats in southern California. These party boats (charging so much per person per day trip) would first fish in the mornings to catch bait, and then go farther offshore so that their paying customers could go after the big fish. These boats would come back in time to report their catches for next-day publication in the local newspaper. These reports bragged about the big fish they had caught as a means of attracting anglers for the next day's trip. After stints in the Navy and as a park technician in the Virgin Islands, Davis came back to southern California fifteen years later. The party boat process was the same, except that the bragging in the local newspapers was now about having caught what used to be the bait fish! The big fish were gone.

Baselines had changed. If you never saw how things were, you are often happy with what little you now see. And you wouldn't know how incredible things could be again.

A prime example of the danger of euphemisms has been the Marine Sanctuary Program of the National Oceanic and Atmospheric Administration (NOAA). Once (in 2000), when NOAA's lack of fisheries management authority in marine sanctuaries was receiving intense media scrutiny, NOAA felt the need to assess its performance and also enhance its public image. One attempt to build credibility (and shore up public confidence) was to convene a National Academy of Public Administration panel to provide a study of NOAA's Marine Sanctuary Program.[17]

During the panel's early deliberations, top marine experts sat around a conference table and listened to NOAA's presentation. At one point, a wise and wizened Australian scientist, sensing a whiff of "smoke and mirrors," asked, with a twinkle in his eye: "If I were a fish, what would it mean to me to find myself in a marine sanctuary?" Spontaneously, someone in the room blurted out, "Better swim like hell!" The truth, apparently, will always out.

It is not due to chance or agency ineptitude that NOAA's network of national marine sanctuaries provides little sanctuary or real protection for most of the marine life that one would assume was protected in a marine "sanctuary." While affording some control over submerged pipelines, mining, and shipping routes, lack of protection from commercial fishing was built into the system, in many cases as a means to placate the interests that want few restrictions on access to ocean resources. Marine sanctuaries—if they do not restrict fishing—are protected areas largely in name only and provide a false sense of protection. This is so at a time when our nation's fisheries, like the world's fisheries, have been decimated.

In many ways the National Park Service has not done any better for its fish. Politics have caused park fisheries' control to be ceded to state management and regulations. Even with well-protected habitats and water quality, state fish and game agencies' approaches to regulating fishing have proved inadequate to sustain wild life populations and unimpaired ecosystems in parks. Decades of research and monitoring have revealed that the condition of fishery resources in marine parks is roughly the same as that outside parks: they are severely depleted. The ecological effects of collapsed fish populations cascade through parks as everywhere else, threatening the ecological community's structure and ecosystem health. The long-term consequence has been to impair aquatic wild life and, for those who fish or dive, degrade the overall park experience.

It is time to recognize the serial collapse of commercial fish species for the major ecological disruption it is: perhaps the last dying vestige of the expectations that launched the fantasy of inexhaustible "food from the sea." It is also time to make hard decisions that orchestrate the use of the ocean's resources in ways that make long-term sense. We must start with zoning our uses within our country's Exclusive Economic Zone (the subsurface resources out to two hundred nautical miles offshore) in ways compatible with the spawning and life histories and longevities of both fish and their complete communities. It is past time to exclude some selected areas from the intense harvesting regimes that new technology (better boats, navigation, and gear) has unleashed. Without such a strategic response, our fisheries at large, as well as those protected under the American covenant, will be seriously—and possibly irretrievably—broken in marine and marine-linked natural systems.

The opportunities for better management measures are well understood by the scientific community, and a plan to manage wisely is easily within reach. Regrettably, worldwide there is no source of leadership with enough authority to counter the current trends in ocean decline. At the national level, the best first step is for each maritime nation to build its own representative system of marine protected areas, complete with no-take zones that not only preserve complex marine communities but act as recharge engines supplying larvae and adults that sustain fisheries outside the strategically placed protection zones. There is evidence that this works from recent success stories coming from both NOAA and the NPS (as well as from other zoning efforts springing up around the world—some instigated by fishermen).

After great investment in involving the public in California and the Florida Keys, a truly enlightened approach to zoning parts of sanctuary and park waters has resulted in "no-take" zones at Dry Tortugas and Channel Islands National Parks and their adjacent NOAA marine sanctuaries. These limited fishing zones truly give refuge to fish and marine species that can now live long enough to have the reproductive potential necessary to maintain their populations. And despite resistance from special interests, they are working as hoped.

Issues of control and protection within the current national marine parks are relatively easy to address compared to establishing any new area that would eliminate commercial or recreational fishing. In our current national parks, opportunities abound—implementation is a matter of political will and enlightened leadership.

Gary Davis's career spanned a remarkable time both for the National Park Service's marine programs and for the resources he has studied. As a park ranger, graduate student, and researcher, then the National Park Service's leading voice for prudent management of ocean resources, he has been an eyewitness to the dramatically shifting baselines of the ocean's fisheries and in particular the marine resources of national park units. Davis provides an invaluable perspective on the status of marine resources in the National Park System. His work in Virgin Islands National Park provides an overview that only long-term observation (like that of Dr. Bill in the Everglades) can provide.

Early surveys (from the 1960s) of ocean wild life in Virgin Islands National Park and Buck Island Reef National Monument, also in the Virgin Islands, recorded abundant large groupers and snappers, lobsters, and conch. Local fishermen could feed their families and meet the demands for fresh seafood of local resorts by snorkeling in shallow water and using traditional woven arrowhead traps to catch big predatory fish. Fifty years later, fish traps catch only small herbivores. Mature conch and lobster are rarely seen, even in deep water, and resorts import frozen seafood from afar. Scientists surveying fish populations now search for weeks to find a single small grouper. Recreational and artisanal fishing eventually removed most large reef predators and grazers, allowing algae to increase and compete with corals for light and space. The ecological effects of fishing down the food pyramid, combined with runoff from human-altered local watersheds (increasing sediments and nutrients), have resulted in critical levels of environmental stress for reef-building corals.

The combined stresses appear to have impaired the corals' immune systems and made them more sensitive to global forces such as warming sea temperatures and susceptible to previously unknown diseases. In 2005 warm water caused nearly 60 percent of reef corals at park study sites to die, some directly from thermal stress and others from subsequent diseases months later.[18] A cascade of these interdependent stress factors further diminished the reefs' resilience to normal hurricane disturbances, exacerbating an already precarious situation for park reefs.

Hundreds of species of park wild life depend exclusively on these reefs for food, shelter, and other life essentials. Two major western Atlantic reef-building corals, elkhorn and staghorn (*Acropora palmata* and *A. cervicornis*), were designated in 2006 as "threatened" under the U.S. Endangered Species Act. The coral reef chain of life is stretched dangerously thin in Virgin Islands parks, with many links poised to fail.

While the peril here is clear, the opportunity is also clear because issues in established national parks can be addressed with steadfast and bold leadership. What does a future with the covenant intact look like for our ocean heritage?

- A fully protected and representative set of marine reserves with spectacular features and wild life just as iconic as those of Grand Canyon, Yellowstone, and Yosemite NPs. These will be increasingly accessible because of advancing ocean technology.
- Marine reserves that serve as refuges, illustrate the natural bounty of our oceans, and replenish fishing stocks beyond their boundaries.
- Wilderness areas in ocean parks that serve as living laboratories that inform, inspire, and reward people, encouraging them to be better stewards of nature.

These goals, well within reach, will, however, rapidly slip away; windows of opportunity are wide but closing. If park policies on managing marine fish are not changed decisively now, with broad and persistent public support, no subsequent generation will have the option to enjoy fishing or know the sea as earlier generations have experienced it. Along with bison herds and giant sequoias, we must not lose the wonder and beauty of coral reefs, kelp forests, and big fish.

In the Gulf of Maine, where fishing pressure has been intense and the rate of warming appears to be rapid, adding a New England offshore "emerald necklace" system of national monuments (similar in concept to what Frederick Law Olmsted crafted with city parks for Boston) would give permanent protection to key spawning and nursery areas and shallow seamounts like Cashes Ledge. Oceanographer Sylvia Earle calls Cashes Ledge the "Yellowstone of the North Atlantic." In 2016 President Obama created the first marine national monument in the Atlantic Ocean (Northeast Canyon and Seamounts Marine National Monument), but efforts to make Cashes Ledge a national monument failed.

Irreplaceable habitats critical to the integrity, stability, and beauty of our ocean parks require a new era of seizing opportunities for science-based care to protect and recover the bounty of our coastal waters in new marine parks. This should include renewed efforts to add jewels such as Cashes Ledge to the nation's protected heritage.

Other Opportunities

On land, an example of both the perils and the opportunities regarding the National Park System in modern times recently played out in the north woods of Maine. Until recently, northern forests had not been well represented in the National Park System, and conservationists had long pushed for a national park in Maine's north woods, some advocating for up to 3 million of the state's 17 million acres of forest. A plan of this magnitude created strong opposition locally, with elected officials at the county and state levels and with most of Maine's members of Congress.

We have a world-class system of national parks partly because there have been many successful people throughout history who have wanted to leave a legacy that benefits both people and nature in perpetuity. Entrepreneur Roxanne Quimby, co-founder of Burt's Bees and a great fan of national parks, wished to create a national park with over 80,000 acres of her own land for the people of this nation and Maine. There was much local angst about taking away timber acreage, even though her plan amounted to less than 1 percent of the 17 million acres once controlled by the declining forest products industry, which had been selling off its lands and dismantling its mills. The bigger issue for local Mainers may have been their fear of losing the kinds of recreational access traditionally allowed by the timber industry. Curiously, some Mainers seem to jealousy guard their own private property but have grown addicted to accessing the private property of others. For them, letting the federal government control any land in northern Maine was somehow unacceptable.

Quimby was determined to make this gift of her own property, but after several interviews about her views on certain aspects of life in Maine that didn't go over well with many Mainers, she wisely turned the effort over to her son, Lucas St. Clair. St. Clair made great headway in building support by talking with locals "over a thousand cups of coffee." Still Maine senators, a congressman, and other elected local officials withheld support. Eventually an offer was made to the Obama administration to donate over 87,000 acres of Quimby's land plus an additional gift of $40 million to set up park operations. President Obama declared the gifted land the North Woods and Waters National Monument in 2016, using his authority under the Antiquities Act of 1906.

One important aspect of this example is that nowhere in the discussions among Mainers, or among Maine's political leadership, was there any apparent sense of obligation to see Maine's North Woods proudly represented in the nation's system of natural heritage. Most Mainers probably care strongly about visiting protected elements of the nation's heritage in other states, but others prefer that these protected areas be "not in my backyard." This common response is a perilous barrier to the opportunities and generosity that exist for holding onto our shared heritage.

Another, famous, example of antipathy to protecting national treasure lands occurred during the attempt decades ago to add lands to Grand Tetons National Park. Opposition was intense from local cattlemen, including Senator Cliff Hansen. Hansen and other ranchers once drove a cattle herd through downtown Jackson Hole to dramatically protest the expansion and to stop President Franklin Roosevelt from designating a national monument at Jackson Hole in 1943. Decades later he freely admitted he was "dead wrong" and stated, "That was one battle I'm glad I lost."[19]

Similarly, Totch Brown of Chokoloskee, Florida, rued the day Everglades National Park crimped his lifestyle and ended his career poaching alligators, fishing, and living free in the untamed Everglades. But his memoirs tell about his revelations decades later: "Maybe the park people saw better than I did, that the developers, the retirees, and the sport fishermen might have soon gobbled up most of the mangrove swamps and mud flats, plus every darn piece of shell land high enough to stand on without getting your feet wet. Today this country probably would've been covered with everything from shacky sport-fishing camps to the tallest of high-rises and condos. Most likely, their laws and regulations would've been harder on us natives than the rules of the park. . . . In fact, those of us who stayed would probably have ended up as bellhops in a hotel. Maybe the time for us had simply run out."[20]

Every generation must live in its own times, finding a way past perils while seizing new opportunities. A visit to the Grand Tetons or the Everglades will attest that a representative system of national parks is a treasured legacy for each of us and every generation to strive to leave behind. Seizing new opportunities can strengthen our resolve and fulfill the promise of the national parks in the future of our nation.

Florissant Fossil Beds National Monument.
A key element in successful park management is continuous investment in
science staff for the long-term accumulation and synthesis of basic data into
usable knowledge. (Courtesy of the U.S. National Park Service)

7

Correcting Course

America needs a National Park Service ready for tomorrow. Present and future perils and opportunities require the NPS to act in creative, decisive, and effective ways in order to pass America's covenant on to future generations. The days when it sufficed to provide comfortable visitor services and have worthy generalist rangers watch over resources are gone. Success in protecting our national parks and passing them forward unimpaired will require stellar efforts from a highly sophisticated and professional NPS. To have national parks unimpaired will require a singular vision resolutely shared by the executive branch of our government and Congress in the face of global-scale changes, outside-the-park threats, and entrenched interests. This will require engagement across the entire spectrum of the American public, and it will require leadership from all who have the resources (intellectual, technical, and financial) to push national heritage protection to its highest calling.

These are not trivial or easily met requirements. Each requires surmounting long traditions, negative precedents, locked-in mindsets, and institutional inertia. The difficulties of inter- and intra-organizational change grow with size and complexity, so we begin with a discussion of the retooling needed within the National Park Service.

Future success starts with broadening the agency's culture to include the attributes necessary to achieve its mission in times of rapid change. This, too, is not easily done, nor is it likely to be lasting unless extraordinary steps are taken. Such steps will not likely come from within the NPS. We have learned this from experience, with successes and setbacks. Here are some of the approaches we believe are most needed.

Science for Parks, Parks for Science

An example of resistance to change is reflected in the NPS history of scientific capability and the role of science in parks. In the last half of the twentieth century over a dozen authoritative critiques exposed the need for an appropriate presence and role for science in national parks. These critiques were most often prompted by significant, widely reported, and embarrassing failures that resulted from not understanding the fundamentals of natural resources issues.

In 1963, the National Academy of Sciences' National Research Council found: "It is inconceivable to this Committee that property so unique and valuable as the national parks, used by such a large number of people, and regarded internationally as one of the finest examples of our national spirit, should not be provided with sufficient competent research scientists in natural history as elementary insurance for the preservation and best use of parks." They added: "The Committee was shocked to learn that for the year 1962 the research staff (including the Chief Naturalist and field men in natural history) was limited to 10 people and that the Service budget for natural history research was $28,000—about the cost of one campground comfort station."[1]

By 1992, not much had changed. The National Research Council's Committee on Improving the Science and Technology Programs of the National Park Service observed: "With the 20/20 vision of hindsight, any examination of the national park system can uncover many cases in which a lack of understanding of park resources has led to problems—degradation of resource quality, increased conflicts between visitors and resources, or the escalation of minor issues into major problems."[2]

Also, "Since the first major independent reviews of the adequacy of the National Park Service science program were conducted in the early 1960s, many experts have shared their views on the scope and quality of the National Park Service research program. In all, the many reviews provide both general and very specific recommendations for strengthening science in support of the parks. Many of the suggested improvements were recommended repeatedly, yet few have been effectively or consistently implemented." And, in further testament to the difficulty of organizational change: "Indeed, many administrations have come and gone during the past 30 years and they have operated in very different settings, but with the same result—science has not taken hold as a key element in the foundation of the National Park Service mission."[3] These assessments were repeated in the Second Century Commission's report in 2009 and the National Park System Advisory Board's report *Revisiting Leopold* in 2011.

The key point again is the lack of a real understanding by NPS leadership of the need for long-term accumulation of scientific data and competency in its application. That begins with awareness and appreciation of science and the role science must play in park management.

Over the past few decades, the occurrence of controversial issues involving natural resources has become more and more frequent and time-consuming for park management. A superintendent once complained accusingly to Mike (when Mike had taken on overall responsibility for natural resource management in parks), "If it weren't for natural resource issues I could manage my park." Perhaps the superintendent meant that he could get on with managing visitor services if the plants and animals stayed put, stayed healthy, and did not act up.

Embarrassing failures in managing Yellowstone elk and bison herds, including overgrazing followed by massive cullings, had become front-page news by the 1960s. The NPS grudgingly began to accept the need for basic science, but only that which answered the most immediate questions vexing superintendents.

Faced with immediate crises, superintendents often remained bewildered by some of the answers coming from the scientists. Most natural resource systems are complicated by many variables, and without data sets over multiple seasons, scientists must couch their answers with caveats conveying the uncertainty that exists from short-term study of long-term phenomena. It is that issue that leads managers, upon hearing "On the one hand . . ., while on the other hand . . .," to famously ask in desperation if someone could please find a one-armed biologist.

The presence of either NPS or external scientists in parks has not been traditionally supported. Indeed, George Menendez Wright, the Service's first chief scientist, had to draw on his own personal fortune to build the Service's first science program in the 1930s. Upon his tragic death in 1935, the science program promptly disappeared; the general antipathy toward science persisted to some degree throughout the twentieth century.

Bill Briggle, a legendary and traditional park ranger who became a powerful superintendent and for a time was in charge of all park operations across the Service, once opined that he didn't want a host of scientists with butterfly nets running through his parks doing "hobby science." His opinion became known as "Briggle's Rule," which dictated that no research was to be supported in any park unless it was immediately applicable to the superintendent's most pressing current issues.

One problem with "Briggle's Rule" is that many park issues have to be addressed immediately due to public or congressional pressure, budget request cycles, or project planning schedules. If money was found to initiate a study of a resource issue, the research usually took several years to get enough seasonal data to know what was going on and then a year to make sense of it and have a necessary peer review of the study results. By that time, the issue had often been decided, the superintendent had taken action, and the result was being lived with. Beginning a study after an issue arises simply does not work. And trying to predict the issues of the future is also problematic. As the National Research Council noticed, there were frequently regrettable outcomes from such a "tacked-on," or "brush-fire," role for science in parks.

For example, in Everglades NP there was often a sense of satisfaction as the staff turned down persistent research permit applications from a University of Miami expert in bee ecology. Each year he would ask to have access to the Everglades National Park to study the native bee community. "Not close to being a priority," the park staff would opine, thereby saving the small amount of time they would have to spend on hosting the study. Then one day "Africanized bees" were discovered making their way across the Gulf states to South Florida. The intense media coverage included speculation that these hybridized "killer bees" would find a home and safe haven in the Everglades from which to attack Miami. Would the native population be resilient enough to maintain themselves against this new invader? In fact, were there native bees in the Everglades? If so, would they further hybridize with the aggressive "killer bee" strain? The park had no answers at all about bees. With hat (and research permit) in hand, park staff hastily went off to find the University of Miami professor.

For many years park superintendents resisted the idea of spending operational funds on scientific studies. They justified this reluctance based on the rationale that the terms "science" and "research" were not specifically mentioned in the NPS Organic Act. Yet they were coming up short in hotly contested resource issues. Sometimes an appearance in court and cross-examination was required to convert park managers to the utility of deep resource knowledge. More and more often these appearances became public meetings demanding answers as to why some management actions were being taken, or not. A number of court decisions, including some that temporarily replaced the superintendent's jurisdiction with court authority, added to the increasing awareness in the NPS of the need for better science. Tellingly, the Department of the Interior solicitor whose job it was to defend the NPS in the courtroom told NPS leadership at the turn of the millennium that his office would not continue to represent the NPS if it didn't have a strong administrative record demonstrating that decisions were being made on a sound scientific basis. He was tired of losing.

At other times the NPS suffered from the inability to convince another agency to modify its proposed projects (from clear-cuts along the parks' boundaries to building dams upstream from the parks) to make them more compatible with the long-term health of a national park. In a well-known example, astronauts in space wondered aloud about the strange green squares that they could see standing alone in the western U.S. landscape. They looked like postage stamps. They were actually western parks surrounded by National Forests where the U.S. Forest Service had clear-cut the timber right up to the park boundary. This practice effectively isolates a park in a fashion similar to girdling a tree by removing its bark. Yet the practice was fully compatible with U.S. Forest Service policies at the time.

These negative experiences were gradually driving many individual park superintendents to support science in parks, but the fact that the Organic Act didn't specifically mention research remained a problem. In 1998 Senator Craig Thomas (R) from Wyoming called a Senate hearing at which he asked NPS representatives how the NPS could manage 80-plus million acres spread across 270 different units, with eighty resource parks that had no resource managers with even a basic bachelor of science degree. There was no answer. Senator Thomas followed up by including a "research mandate" in his National Parks Omnibus Management Act of 1998 (also known as the "Thomas

Bill"). This bill had been requested by the Department of the Interior to solve issues stemming from park concession contracts to provide visitor services. Against Interior's wishes (but with NPS background support), Thomas added language directing the secretary of the Interior to continually improve the National Park Service's ability to provide and demonstrate the scientific basis for its management, protection, and interpretation of park resources. A key element was formal authorization to create the Cooperative Ecosystem Studies Unit Network, the federal–university science partnership that Gary led and now includes over four hundred U.S. universities.

In addition, Title II of the Act included authority to "enhance protection and management of the national park resources by providing clear authority and direction for the scientific study in the National Park System and to use the information gathered for management purposes." It went on to add encouragement to others to use the National Park System for study that would benefit park management and have broader scientific value, where such study is consistent with the Organic Act. The "Thomas Bill" also provided steps for achieving this, including comprehensive training for all employees to ensure that they are equipped with "the best, up-to-date knowledge, skills, and abilities" to protect park resources.

This all meant several important things, including that, as of 1998, scientists with "butterfly nets" were now officially welcome, as long as their activities were compatible with the long-term health of park resources. This should have ended "Briggle's Rule." Yet much of that attitude remains, and many park staffs still fend off outside researchers. Sometimes it is warranted, as when the research would modify or remove (by collecting samples or specimens) park resources to an unacceptable degree. More often parks would just rather not have the additional workload of having to issue permits in a timely fashion and host outsiders in sometimes difficult terrain. At the Everglades, Mike was able to hire a full-time liaison who kept visiting researchers from getting snake-bit or stranded at night in uncomfortable or unsafe circumstances.

Overall, the solution to the problem of obtaining the necessary scientific data for parks lies in a change in mindset to one that embraces the concept of "parks for science, science for parks"—that is, promoting parks as laboratories hosting long-term studies that provide usable knowledge for park managers and can contribute to the advance of science.

A Step in the Right Direction

It is important that parks be seen—by park staff, national leadership, Congress, and academe—as natural laboratories that are national assets. Picture a national park established a hundred years ago that had systematically welcomed scientists from its beginning. It is easy to coax researchers to work in national parks because of what they offer on often-dramatic research sites and issues, the relative safety of research sites and equipment from vandalism or removal, and the possibility of seeing their work reflected in concrete management actions for the public good. A park that consistently welcomed researchers would have soon developed a vibrant community of researchers, students, and volunteers that would in some cases have focused their entire careers on park ecosystems.

That unfortunately imaginary park—though a few have been blessed with a long history of academic interest, and a few more have historically maintained some scientist staff—would have benefited from a slowly but steadily growing wealth of information, usable knowledge, and overall understanding of its resources. The resulting park research community and the park's data-rich context would have attracted an increasingly broad spectrum of subject-matter experts eager to use the park as a foundation for their studies in their own specialties. Their students, often from local areas, typically do much of the research work. They become engaged in park issues and are often the best spokespeople in local arenas.

Each new researcher with his or her own specialty would add a missing piece to the park's conceptual model of how park ecosystems function. Over time the model would be refined and revised with processes, rates, and relationships important to understanding the dynamics of park ecosystems, and at some point it would become testable for answering real-world questions. That hypothetical park's staff, rich in usable knowledge and advantaged by an engaged research community, would be able to tell compelling stories and answer questions authoritatively. Over time, the park's staff would become a reliable, trusted source of knowledge on environmental issues and also provide inspirational outreach, education, and conservation leadership.

The park's staff would also have immediate access to expert opinions from researchers who would have spent, in some cases, decades unraveling the intricacies of the park's ecology. Year after year, the information could have been assimilated and integrated into the mix of what is known about the park and how effectively it is being protected. The growing understanding and knowledge base, if incorporated into the park's interpretive education effort, would enhance support through education for long-term park protection in local communities, visitors, and the public at large. To achieve this takes a commitment to allocating resource management staff time and usually some workspace and bunk space to build a community of researchers. Often researchers bring their own grant money and talented, hardworking graduate students.

Such ideas were incorporated in 1999 into a substantial program aimed at broadening the culture of the NPS toward a vision for its success in the twenty-first century. The initiative was called the Natural Resource Challenge (NRC). The NRC was conceived and launched in response to a mounting range of criticism of park management, thoroughly documented in a pivotal book by Richard Sellars, *Preserving Nature in the National Parks.* His first edition, published in 1997, was an intensely detailed chronicle of the agency's failure to embrace science as a fundamental necessity for achieving its mission.[4] Along with the need to deal with the expected criticism from the book's message, there was a growing willingness among top NPS leaders to take steps to position national parks to squarely face the ominous and uncertain future that the twenty-first century seemed to promise. The NPS director, Bob Stanton, and his leadership team were proud of the NPS's overall history of success but also wanted to ensure that the NPS culture would adapt toward what it must become to be successful in meeting the highly technical challenges it was so likely to confront in the future.

The Natural Resource Challenge included the Research Learning Center concept (manifested in the network of nineteen centers), Cooperative Ecosystem Studies units, a strategic approach to completing inventories of vascular plants and vertebrate species, and a "park vital signs" monitoring effort in 270 natural resource parks. Other steps included the development of fast online research permit applications, a new ocean science program effort, a national cave management program, a Cave and Karst research center, a Night Sky program, a Natural Sounds program, a Social Science program, and Exotic Plant Management teams (circuit riders used to control invasive plants at a range of western parks). While the funding level reached only four-fifths of the overall request to Congress, over five hundred science positions were added to the NPS, and the expenditure of every dollar as well as progress was reported back to Congress each year. This new momentum for science attracted outside funding for a Park Flight Migratory Bird program (funded by American Airlines), a Mellon Foundation postdoctoral fellowship program in plant community dynamics, and the Canon National Parks Science Scholars program, which funded seventy-nine graduate students to enable them to do their dissertation research in national parks. A *Year-in-Review* annual report was published for ten years to display the breadth of the resource challenges faced by parks—documenting resource protection victories as well as defeats—and distributed to congressional staff and the public.

Many felt great pride in this attempt to address the historic imbalances and lack of focus on resources by an agency with such heavy resource management responsibilities. Others also felt that it was just phase one and that there was much more to be done.

However, rather than building on this start, there are signs that the NPS and national parks are reverting to their familiar default mode: visitor services. Positions allocated to the Research Learning Center network have disappeared. Regional chief scientist positions have vanished. The Park Flight position has vanished. The Canon National Parks Science Scholars program has ended, and the travel funds that allow the circuit-riding Exotic Plant Management Teams to cover a range of parks have at times been frozen. The cooperative agreement mechanisms that allow for partnerships with academe and other support organizations have been overburdened with paperwork and undermined by political review. The NPS has failed to fill the position of science adviser to the director.

Problematically, even when resources are provided directly by Congress for specific activities, national park managers have great latitude in how they spend park budget increases—no matter what they were intended for in the original budget request. So with that latitude, priorities eventually become matters of comfort zones. The daily press of visitor and facilities management pressures chips away at long-term resource programs for the immediate gratification that comes from providing visitor services. Deputy Director Galvin once explained this bowing to the pressures of the moment as due to the fact that "bears don't phone their Congressman." After twenty years, that process appears to be eroding what progress has been made with the NRC initiative.

Without deep organizational change, the NPS will easily slide back into being the custodian for, not the authority on, its natural resources and their protection.

Park Leadership That Leads

A lasting attitude shift must start with park superintendents. They are the leadership core of the National Park Service, holding great power over many aspects of park management. Traditionally rangers formed "the feeder group" for superintendents, and superintendents formed the feeder group for policy-level leadership and sometimes National Park Service directors. In the future, the NPS director should ideally have either a background in or at least comfort with science. Although the director need not be a scientist, he or she must know the value of scientific thinking and data, have basic science skills, and know how to make use of scientific staff. There is a myth, although with some basis, that scientists cannot be good managers or politicians. Accordingly, many believe that, as Churchill said: "Scientists should be on tap, not on top." Suffice it to say that a national park director or park manager must have a wide range of skills but, at the very least, as the manager of invaluable natural resources, ought to be comfortable with the basics of science and view the advice of scientists in at least as serious a vein as they would counsel from members of the legal profession.

Because the issues and decisions facing contemporary NPS directors are so complex and the need for science-informed decisions so great, along with the inevitable tendency in government agencies for division and for program leaders to defend their turf and advocate for more funding, the NPS director needs access to unfettered scientific advice. The position of science adviser to the director should become a formal part of every future director's leadership team.

Interestingly, the Second Century Commission's Committee on Natural Resources recommended that the NPS director (or at least the deputy director) be selected for his or her potential to serve on the president's science advisory committees, such as the National Science and Technology Council, or in the Office of Science and Technology Policy.[5] This, among other things, would symbolize and elevate the role of parks in protecting our national heritage into a venue that determines national priorities.

Today national park rangers have become a less dominant feeder group for park superintendent positions. The early park ranger mold was that of a self-reliant generalist, capable of whatever the task at hand required, while intimately conversant with nature and the backcountry. In the last half of the twentieth century, this romantic role (and image) morphed somewhat to a role with a heavier emphasis on law enforcement. Whether this stark transformation from benevolent authority figure into heavily armed Kevlar-vested police made complete sense or not, it happened quickly and without much evaluation as to its effect on the agency's mission.

There is no doubt that many parks bear the burden of severe law enforcement challenges (along the borders, in areas with high levels of drug trafficking, and in some urban parks). The reality is that there have been many deadly instances in which undertrained and outgunned park rangers have been up against hardened criminals in parks across the United States, and even members of drug cartels along the southwest border.

Surprisingly there is evidence that national park rangers are among the most assaulted law enforcement officers in our nation.[6] One might ask why that is. Could it be that law enforcement training and the consequent mindset do not conform to the public's expectations of the traditional ranger-naturalist? Law enforcement can be a noble and often thankless task, and it will be a challenge to shape the law enforcement approach to accommodate the range of general to specialized tasks at hand in every park.

In Florida's Big Cypress National Preserve, beginning in the 1980s a local university professor devoted much of his career to understanding the ecology of the preserve's rich reptile community. He placed radio tracking devices on diamondback rattlers to understand their seasonal movements (which correspond with changing water levels). He also focused on understanding the fate of alligators in the changing hydrology of Everglades NP and Big Cypress National Preserve. One dark night while he and several graduate students were tagging alligators in the middle of Big Cypress, they were surprised by the sudden appearance of a flashlight beam and an assault rifle pointed at them. They dropped the alligator and raised their hands. The person behind the assault rifle identified himself as a park ranger (he was a new hire from the Miami-area police force). The professor explained that they were researchers engaged in a long-term study of alligator population movements, under a research permit from the park. He asked if he could find the permit in his vest; the ranger lowered his gun, took the permit, and examined it. "Hold on a minute! This permit's expired," he said snapping the loaded assault rifle back up to cover them. That professor and his crew never worked in a park again.

Many superintendents have pushed back on the heavy law enforcement image of rangers in their parks, even if it is only to direct that shotguns are not to be mounted on the dashboards of ranger vehicles so that they are not the first thing a parks visitor sees when asking for directions. The intense training required each year to maintain credentials, and the inexorable shift in mindset from facilitating park visits to looking for infractions and confronting criminals, have had a significant effect on NPS priorities and staffing.

This is important because the drift of park rangers to law enforcement has had another unforeseen outcome. Federal law enforcement officers are eligible for retirement at age fifty-five after twenty years of service or at any age with twenty-five years of service. This has led to some diminishment of the traditional feeder group for the superintendent ranks. Whereas many field rangers came from backgrounds in resources, today's superintendents are most likely to be drawn from a wider array of backgrounds, but seldom for comfort with, if not mastery of, the science that should underpin each park resource decision.

As resource threats increase, park managers should be able to speak authoritatively on park resources, not just be caretakers. To be successful in protecting parks, park superintendents must be actively engaged in working outside park boundaries—providing a vision of the benefits of long-term park health and its associated quality of life in surrounding communities. Those candidates who are chosen for experience or leadership qualities but who have no backgrounds in or comfort with science must be given effective training on the appreciation and conditions needed for building a science-based foundation for park management. As required in the now politically rescinded Director's Order 100, a minimum science literacy should be required of all candidates for a superintendency. At the very least, superintendents should be capable of ensuring that a science foundation is accumulated and assimilated into park planning, interpretation, and regional outreach. Improving regional and local planning is a strong investment in long-term park health as well as the quality of life in surrounding communities.

Parks do not often have superintendents who understand the importance of investing in science, much less an unbroken succession of superintendents who are committed to this investment. In 2004 Mike attended the book fair associated with a national geological conference and was pleased to find a beautiful new book that synthesized what was known about the fossils of Florissant Fossil Beds National Monument.[7] Florissant is a remarkable site in Colorado that protects the fossils of a redwood forest smothered by mud flows from a "Mount St. Helens–like" volcano that erupted 34 million years ago. The author had sought out, compiled, and synthesized all that was known from the fossils that had been collected from Florissant by paleontologists for over a hundred years. Many fossils had been placed in museums from Berkeley to London. The author, an employee at Florissant, had produced the authoritative synthesis—elevating the NPS from caretaker to world's authority on its park resources. On being congratulated for his achievement, and for his diligence in staying in a park long enough to become the authority on it, the author said he regrettably couldn't stay much longer. With children heading for college he couldn't continue at the park on his G-11 salary—a level that was usually below the entry-level salary of a PhD in academe. There was no career ladder for him in the park. Earlier pay-scale adjustment programs such as Research Grade Evaluation had been available to establish park scientists' pay based on their level of scientific contribution. That enabled park researchers to have a career ladder without jumping to bigger parks or universities. This encouraged long-term intimacy with park resources but was lost with the creation of the National Biological Survey in 1992.

As luck would have it, the acting superintendent of Florissant National Monument was also at this conference. When asked if there was a way to develop a career ladder in the park for this park scientist, his response was that there was no need and certainly no chance, as the scientist was already being paid the same as his chief of maintenance. The maintenance of visitor-service infrastructure (often managing and maintaining facilities in accordance with local building codes) is thus equated in importance by some of our brightest superintendents to being the world's authority on the resources for which the park was established.

There is a strong case to be made for the important potential contributions of each park staff member and most certainly those in the maintenance division. They can be leaders in developing environmentally sensitive approaches to visitor facilities and park operations. In 1996 the Natural Resource Stewardship and Science Division expanded a series of national-level awards that included a Director's Award for Excellence in Resource Management through Maintenance, along with Superintendent, Resource Manager, and Scientist awards. One of the most moving acceptance speeches over ten years of award ceremonies came from a Hawaiian park's heavy equipment operator who had developed phenomenal skill in bulldozing invasive plants from sensitive plant communities with surgical precision. He understood the fragility of the resource and the "honor" it was to contribute to its protection. There should be a national competition and prize for the best draft of "Surgical Methods for Maintenance Operations in National Parks."

Nevertheless, the training, devotion, and commitment required to become an authority on the resources a park was designated to protect should merit sufficient salary and respect to attract and retain their service, as well as scientific credibility onsite in parks.

Missed Opportunities

If we as a species are asking for too much from the earth, then something has to change. Change begins with awareness. With over 100 million visitors each year, national parks can influence a lot of thinking and perhaps even lifestyles. One popular image associated with national parks is that of the self-reliant ranger living light on the land. Chat rooms, and even street corners, are full of people either fantasizing or actively seeking to abandon their current lifestyle in favor of a back-to-nature profession and a simpler life. Parks are indeed great places to escape the material world if indeed they do not become overdeveloped and wasteful. Park facilities can either demonstrate a new environmental ethic or merely deliver the status quo in a pristine setting.

When assisting South Africa's Working for Water Program, Gary and Mike noticed some interesting water conservation approaches that made great sense. With the fall of apartheid, there was much work to do in providing basic services, including potable water systems, to those who had had so few. South Africa was building water conservation principles into its development projects. Taking back home ideas learned from South Africa related to water awareness and conservation and applying them proved impossible, even when the Albright Training Center at Grand Canyon National Park was undergoing a major renovation. There, at the main ranger training facility in the United States, was an opportunity to introduce water-saving technologies in a training context, and even in a research context—measuring water use among groups and against other variables. The south rim of the Grand Canyon has so little water that it has had to pipe its water from the north rim down the canyon and across the Colorado River and then up to the south rim for both park and training center operations. It is the perfect place to attune staff, trainees, and visitors to water conservation habits and techniques. Yet the Department of the Interior and the NPS at all leadership levels showed no interest in water conservation proposals.

Overall, there has been substantial progress in incorporating energy efficiency and sustainable designs into park infrastructure in the past few decades. Some parks have eliminated traffic jams by designing shuttle bus systems, and many have built energy-efficient facilities. Still, a world-class effort and broad consistency in messaging elude the National Park Service. A significant portion of the American population who visit national parks are inspired by nature and open to conservation messages and demonstrated leadership. This presents a major opportunity for the NPS to make a real difference in how we as citizens see and act in the world.

The Case for a Major Organizational Change

For the National Park Service to achieve its potential for protecting the places that shape the American spirit, something fundamental has to change in how it operates. Such change in agency leadership and culture may require converting the NPS to an independent agency. Why would this be?

The National Park Service is currently buried within the Department of the Interior—sometimes called the "department of everything else." It is ironic that a shining star among federal agencies in terms of overall public affection and support is in large part eclipsed within the Department of the Interior. Interior is busy with a broad array of responsibilities for oil, gas, and mineral leasing on its extensive public land holdings and on tribal lands. It contains the Bureau of Ocean Energy Management (offshore drilling) and the Office of Surface Mining. Overall, the Interior secretary manages over 500 million acres of public lands and oversees the trust obligations to Native Americans' lands through the Bureau of Indian Affairs, as well as overseeing far-flung trust territories through the Office of Insular Affairs. When seeking adequate priority for its preservation role, the NPS must compete with over sixty offices with specialized agendas and four bureaus (the Bureau of Reclamation, Bureau of Land Management, Bureau of Indian Affairs, and Bureau of Offshore Energy Management) responsible for "multi-purpose lands"—those yielding gas, oil, minerals, grazing, hydropower, and more. The availability of such commodities from public lands breeds lobbyists who cultivate many friends for these bureaus in Congress. The Fish and Wildlife Service and the U.S. Geological Survey have more compatible missions and similar status in the halls of the Interior building.

While the NPS suffers from a lack of priority and attention in Interior, the department (under both Democratic and Republican administrations) has been aggressive in consolidating central control of basic services—bundling law enforcement, legal support, contracting services, and personnel policies in the office of the secretary in order to apply them in blanket form across the widest spectrum of responsibilities (from Indian gaming to offshore leasing to hydropower development to park protection). Thus, the same administrative practices are applied rather rigidly to widely differing geographic areas and kinds of tasks. In national parks it has become very difficult to hire seasonals, obligate funds in a timely manner, and work effectively with nongovernment partners.

Vested interests can focus their efforts to influence budgetary and regulatory decisions in ways that often catch the American public unaware despite the broad good will and support for the NPS. Agencies and departments whose activities are at times sources of threat to NPS lands, priorities, and budgets include the U.S. Forest Service, the Bureau of Reclamation, the Bureau of Land Management, the Federal Aviation Administration, Homeland Security, and the Army Corps of Engineers. There are constant battles over grazing, hunting, mining, jurisdiction, mines, dams, solar panel arrays, pipeline rights-of-way, states' rights and wildlife, water flow rates, deforestation along park boundaries, and more. Unless issues become widely visible, Congress is likely to side with definable economic interests over incremental impacts to national parks. Countless hours of meetings on issues that drag on for decades in some cases sap the NPS's ability to pursue positive change and organizational improvement. Over the years there have been many great champions who have defended and promoted parks both in the executive branch and in Congress; there are few such advocates for national parks in Washington now.

In this predatory bureaucratic environment, with leadership that varies in its intensity and direction depending on the four-year election cycle, it is a wonder that national parks largely fulfill their mission and the American covenant. Preservation efforts requiring long-term vision and restraint are often undermined by inconsistent support as a result of these political and intra-agency realities. An executive order setting the protection of our natural heritage as a common executive-branch priority—and a corollary to the mission of all federal agencies—would be a simple first step for an incoming president. It would require some demonstration of seriousness by following up on implementation but would send a clear message that this American covenant is for all of us—it's everybody's job—to fulfill.

An even more controversial solution might be to provide greater visibility and autonomy to the National Park System in the federal government's hierarchy as a separate agency. Models might be the National Archives and Records Administration, the Environmental Protection Agency, the National Aeronautics and Space Administration (NASA), the National Science Foundation, or perhaps the Smithsonian Institution model, which allows for great flexibility through a combined public-nongovernment partnership approach. An independent agency—outside of any cabinet-level department—could be overseen by a presidentially appointed commission, with staggered terms to ensure that the oversight function has maximum continuity.

This is an idea that has been around for some time but without a champion willing to take it forward through the arduous gauntlet that any change in Washington must pass. While taking care to appoint a secretary of the interior who would not care about departmental turf, and working with Congress to avoid a surprise, a bold president would do a great service to take this important step. It might free the NPS from its present organizational doldrums and elevate the protection of the nation's natural heritage to the visibility and status that national parks deserve. It might also free the NPS budget from having to compete under the budget caps set in congressional committees wherein an increase in one office budget (such as national parks) means a decrease in the budgets of the other offices under that committee (for example, national wildlife refuges). The National Park Service could then make its own independent case for a budget befitting the services it offers in over four hundred national park units in a more transparent way than is currently possible.

Although there are dangers in being an independent agency, we are betting on the continued, if not increased, value the American public places on its National Park System to ensure strong support. Standalone visibility should help. The current annual budget for the operation of the National Park System is approximately $3 billion, and it has roughly 22,000 employees. It is sobering, by comparison, that the Department of Defense has more than 750,000 civilian employees (that is, not armed service members). The protection of our nation currently costs nearly $700 billion (roughly the Department of Defense's budget) each year. A realistic examination of the National Park System budget needed to achieve the increasingly complex task of protecting 85 million acres of heritage lands (plus the key elements of our cultural landscape) should be carried out, with an eye to the importance of defending our natural heritage in all the ways we have discussed.

Of course there must be a rationale and an accounting for how each dollar is spent and how that expenditure is related to how the agency performs. One could argue that, with high approval ratings, overall agency performance is at a high level. However, while the National Park Service enthusiastically pursues additional funding for its "maintenance backlog," it loses track of what it takes to achieve the primary protection mission of the service. During his campaign for president, for example, George W. Bush committed to doubling the amount to be spent on park resources. This commitment, not atypically, was morphed into spending nearly $3 billion to take care of the service's "maintenance backlog" on its facilities. And when that $3 billion was spent, the Bush administration was stymied when it found that the "maintenance backlog" had grown larger under its watch. A significant portion of future increases—appropriate to needs—should go to professionalization and working on the NPS's "information backlog."

Freeing the Parks from the Entrance Fee

There is a related problem that could be easily solved. The National Park Service receives roughly 8 percent of its annual budget from park entrance fees. The cost of raising this 8 percent (fee collection, training, accounting, fee allocation back to both fee and non-fee parks) cuts into this small return. More important, it changes the nature and relationships of a park visit. "User Pays" thinking makes sense in many cases. It does not when applied to access to shared natural heritage and the American covenant. The fee structure for visiting national parks is reasonable and not unduly burdensome for most. Still, any fee has a deterrent effect and discourages entrance to national parks. For low-income Americans or those in poverty, fees are a barrier that is unacceptable. Fees also "commodify the gate"—a socioeconomic term that means the relationship has been changed from a right to service to a commercial transaction with a number of subtle expectations and warranties that come with providing a service for a fee. Notwithstanding that visitors have already been taxed to support the system, the exclusion of anyone for whom the fee is a barrier does not serve the nation well. A family on an afternoon outing may well find an entrance fee a key factor in deciding whether to make a brief visit to the local national park.

Fee collecting in national parks requires training, hiring, overseeing, and accounting for small fees in hundreds of locations and is a significant drain and distraction in parks. It often annoys locals and contributes to traffic tie-ups at entrance stations in many of the most popular parks. Fees do not cover the maintenance costs in parks—and haven't been available for research studies following restrictions imposed by Congress. Congress has generally wanted fee dollars spent for something tangible, things visitors can see. This has often led to more construction in parks, some that is not a priority and all of it costly to maintain.

A new campaign that establishes that park visits are fee-less would not result in much of a loss to the NPS. And if free entrance were extended to all citizens, it would lead to increased visitation from currently underrepresented segments of our population. In addition, if we invite all citizens of the world to experience our National Park System, as our guests, it would encourage even more foreign visitors and increase our ecotourism share. It might also kindle more support for protecting their national heritage when they return home. The increase in foreign visitation would result in economic gain locally, regionally, and nationally and would far outstrip the importance of the small-percentage net loss to the current National Park Service budget.

While a strong case can be made for the intrinsic value of places that protect nature not just for the element of human enjoyment, there are good reasons for encouraging everyone to visit and enjoy national parks. These experiences are important in enriching people's lives, maintaining national identity, fulfilling the covenant, and maintaining the public support necessary to protect parks unimpaired for the future. A positive outcome from abolishing entrance fees would be for all Americans to feel greater ownership of their national parks. Entrance fees are a bad idea and need to be abolished.

Other Issues

It is crucial that each generation understands that it has a role in maintaining America's covenant within and between generations as embodied in the National Park System. This has been known for some time, and there are partnership-based efforts that seek to get every schoolchild to a park. President Obama's Every Kid in a Park program proved to be immensely popular as an initial introduction to national parks. Some partnerships between parks and school systems (those at Great Smoky Mountains National Park, for example) excel at providing repeated visits to their local national parks over the K–12 years. Early and repeated exposure helps "imprint" kids with both nature and their national heritage. Of course substantial evidence also suggests that national parks are powerful classrooms and compelling natural laboratories. All indications are that nature is a powerful force for improving science interest and education. Enhanced use of parks as classrooms could likely have a significant positive impact on science, technology, engineering, and mathematics (STEM) education. A strong alliance with the Department of Education (with its current annual budget of $77 billion) could help counter the declining interest in the sciences. Currently most kids do not get frequent exposure to national parks, if any at all, due to their locations and especially transportation costs. This would seem a perfect area for increased philanthropic engagement.

Another issue in engaging all Americans is the lag time it takes for new immigrants to avail themselves of the National Park System. It has usually taken immigrants one or two generations to discover and engage. It is important that newer Americans understand their ownership of national parks, and there are often opportunities to hold naturalization ceremonies in national parks. Perhaps again distributing an official and substantial "Owner's Manual for the National Park System" should be a routine part of each park-based swearing-in of each new citizen. And where better than the Statue of Liberty or Ellis Island, the Liberty Bell in Philadelphia, but also Redwood, Tall Prairie, Shenandoah, or Yosemite? The common heritage we all share should be realized, understood, and supported by all—and the sooner, the better.

A major responsibility of new generations will be the growth of the system to make it fully representative of the great American landscape. In the first hundred years there was no consistent strategy for building the National Park System. We have seen that the current system has grown without a consistent vision, plan, or systematic identification of sites necessary to become representative, resilient, and redundant. A representative system requires some of everything of value. Resilience requires adequate size of land parcels and their healthy condition. And redundancy requires that we preserve more than one example of each type of ecosystem.

We saw in chapter 6 an informal inventory of the kinds of remarkable places that represent present-day opportunities for evaluation as important additions to the National Park System. A National Academy of Sciences panel or presidential commission should be asked to identify, based on sound science, the remaining places that should be considered. In the past, many park candidates have been derailed by turf battles among agencies or by local ambivalence or antipathy to a federal presence. There is no defense for the former, and strong local and national leadership can often overcome the latter when park designation is a fair process and makes a positive contribution to local well-being. If we resolve that a true representation of our heritage is a national priority, it can be achieved. Windows of opportunity are closing, so there will be just a very few generations that can accomplish this central task. Every citizen will have to demand park system advocacy from their national leaders.

Of Presidents and Parks

At the national level we have seen many presidents and their administrations fully appreciate that national parks are important and dear to Americans. Many have supported park creation, and many others have seized upon parks as sites to use to gain political advantage, often for announcing programs or policies for which they need to rally patriotic support.

Often White House staffs choose a park emblematic for, or advantageous to, their cause. Sometimes national parks are used to garner general support in a campaign. As mentioned earlier, George W. Bush announced, while campaigning in St. Louis (the jumping-off point for Lewis and Clark's expedition into the western wilderness), that he would double the science effort for national parks. In 2016, President Obama became the first sitting president to visit Yosemite National Park in fifty years.

President Clinton frequently used parks for making significant environmental proposals—sometimes with the good fortune of having a bald eagle fly past at the appropriate phrase (as at Rock Creek Park on Earth Day in 1998). He also was aware of the value of national parks in international relationships.

In 1998 President Clinton facilitated an economic summit of Central American leaders in Costa Rica. He chose to highlight the remarkable national park system developed by the Costa Ricans in part because of the close relationship that system has had with our National Park System. During the summit, Clinton visited Braulio Carrillo National Park—a magnificent site of volcanic mountains with an evergreen tropical rainforest in one of the most rugged regions in the country. Here are found beautiful extinct volcanoes, waterfalls, cloud forests, and the male alder (*Ticodendron* sp.)—a tree first discovered in Costa Rica and named after the national nickname for its people ("Ticos").

The event gave a tremendous boost to Costa Rica's parks. At this event, America's president—the world's most powerful leader—demonstrated respect for national parks as the places that each country has identified as important reflections of their nation's heritage and their identity. Clinton's speech followed those of President José

María Figueres of Costa Rica and a Costa Rican astronaut in the presence of Hillary Clinton and Secretary of State Madeleine Albright. The visibility and importance that accrued to this tropical wetland forest—and to the national park effort of Costa Rica in general—was enormous.

There were good reasons that Costa Rica and its national parks were chosen to be highlighted during Clinton's Central American economic summit. Costa Rica had become a leader in ecotourism and in developing biodiversity science and institutionalizing bioprospecting (the search for useful materials in nature) in a careful and fair manner.

Interestingly, the NPS had played a helpful role in that ascendancy. The relationship with Costa Rica's national park system was partly forged by the impact of two Costa Ricans attending the NPS's International Short Course. From 1972 to 1993, the National Park Service and Parks Canada had jointly sponsored an "International Seminar on National Parks and Equivalent Reserves." This effort, also called the International Short Course (ISC), brought together professional park leaders from around the world and provided them direct access to our national parks and personal experiences with those who operate them. The result was a stronger cadre of park professionals worldwide, many of whom have risen to the highest positions in protected-area management within their homelands or in international organizations.

The ISC often began in Canada and traveled down through a range of intermountain parks, with participants stopping to interact with the leaders and practitioners at each location. The course provided an intense seminar in the realities—successes and failures—of these well-developed protected-area systems and gave participants time to present and contrast their own situations and issues. This course has thus played a part in fostering the establishment and operation of many protected areas worldwide.

The best example of the course's impact may well be the story of two men from Costa Rica, Mario Bosa and Alvaro Ugalde. These two, from opposite political parties, attended the NPS International Short Course in 1968. After the course they visited Yellowstone and Great Smokies NPs and then returned to Costa Rica. There they worked together, with leadership between them switching according to which party was in power. Working together, they established the Costa Rican system of protected areas, now representing roughly 20 percent of the country.[8] That system has been an international leader in innovation, a pioneer in biodiversity science and preservation, and a significant success in providing ecotourism benefits to Costa Rica.

Many graduates of the ISC, such as Boza and Ugalde, to this day ardently attest to the powerful impact the course had on their careers—with many reaching high leadership positions in their own countries. Some have asked that the NPS restore its investment in training international leaders by reviving the International Short Course. The United States, via the NPS, could catalyze a great positive conservation impact from once again responsibly sharing this American idea and the American covenant around the world, to be adapted as needed by the other countries. Re-engagement would also keep America's parks moving forward with fresh ideas and innovations that are being generated in national parks around the world.

Why doesn't every American president routinely ask to visit an iconic national park of each country he or she will visit? That would achieve several things. It would introduce our president to what makes each country unique in nature and culture. And it would add immeasurable prestige to the national park systems in other nations. That certainly happened when Clinton made the effort to speak in the rainforest of Braulio Carrillo NP.

Mike once asked a senior Department of State official about such visits. He responded: "What a good idea! I was station chief in Japan during H. W. Bush's visit there. I just took him to tour the new Toys 'R' Us." What message did that send? Emboldened, Mike took the idea a step further.

By serendipity, Mike had a chance to pitch this idea to Vice President Cheney's staffers in 2003. They were visiting the National Park Service hoping to find ways to help the vice president improve his environmental image. As a conservative westerner, he seemed strong on fly fishing and (famously) hunting, but less so on environmental protection. He was receiving a great deal of criticism in the press. Mr. Cheney's staffers were initially interested in the simple idea and asked for a brief proposal. The proposal and, apparently, interest were soon swept away by the invasion of Iraq. But it's still a good idea, and it would cost little and enhance American leadership in heritage preservation.

In sum, the serious business of park protection requires the best science orchestrated by in-park professionals trained to the highest degree. It cannot be left to generalists. The resource management programs of parks must be upgraded with top-notch scientists who stay in parks for decades building research programs that call on teams of subject-matter experts to create a platform of usable knowledge for decision makers. Rather than fend off outsiders, tomorrow's resource managers should encourage, with support facilities and funds, teams of outside researchers that ask questions, form hypotheses, collect data, and build, test, and refine models that explain the workings of nature in national parks. Onsite information managers must relentlessly ensure that information is captured, organized, assessed, documented, and made accessible to all. The National Park Service must step into the light organizationally, step up professionally, and step outside park boundaries to communicate aggressively.

Superintendents must understand the importance, use, and limitations of the information at hand. Each superintendent should report on the status and trends of park resources and take pride in sharing what is known about his or her park. Parks should be viewed as intellectual hubs attracting people and events, and also as reliable interpreters of issues such as climate change and local as well as global environmental trends. The NPS must ramp up its sharing of experiences—good and bad—far and wide. It must systematically engage with others to meet its mission, at home and abroad.

These are ideas and steps that we think are needed to enable wise national park management, given the reality of dynamic and continuous change during the next century. National Park Service staff must master natural systems ecology and be leaders in recognizing the threats and proper responses as the impacts of humans change the world. In spite of a hundred years of success, this fine agency now requires significant course corrections. By becoming authoritative in its understanding of the resources in its charge, the National Park Service can best teach appreciation for the natural dynamics of those resources and share the lessons necessary to protect those dynamics in parks and beyond. Only then can the American covenant remain unbroken.

Yellowstone National Park.
Natural systems in our national parks, where prey and predator test
each other daily, are invaluable stages for evolution to play out and link
us to where we came from and what is fundamentally important to us.
(Courtesy of the U.S. National Park Service)

8

Why Parks Matter

The national park idea has already changed the world, creating covenants among and across generations, and changed the landscape in many corners of the earth. The idea has proved to be "earthshaking" in the reverse sense that it has led to small corners of quiet harmony with nature in almost every country. Nevertheless, the finest hour of our national parks may be yet to come. It will come when national parks live up to their potential as classrooms and catalysts that prepare us with understanding and acceptance of the need for sweeping change in our attitudes and lifestyles. It had best come well before the limits of human domination of nature are at hand. Reaching such limits will be dangerous.

The realization that we as a species have the capability to disrupt the basic pillars of our life-support system is relatively new. A stark and unmistakable example of the damage we can wreak was the possibility of unleashing a nuclear nightmare during the Cold War. More subtle signals have come from the realization that we have been poisoning the land and the food chain with persistent pesticides to grow more food, and depleting the protective ozone layer of the atmosphere with fluorocarbons to comfort ourselves with air conditioning. We are modifying more than half the earth's surface for our comfort and convenience and homogenizing the world's fauna and flora with our global trade and transportation.[1]

A new and existential threat has emerged as climate change has been altering much (if not all) of the natural and human-dominated world. Rates of change are accelerating, dictating that finding and implementing solutions must keep pace.

There are many science-based signals that suggest human society may approach environmental tipping points long before we reach a common understanding of what's happening and galvanize the necessary will to effect countermeasures. We must keep in mind J. R. McNeill's warning: "What Machiavelli said of affairs of state is doubly true of affairs of global ecology and society. It is nearly impossible to see what is happening until it is inconveniently late to do much about it."[2] We had best not tarry in responding to these indications and trends and begin to take positive steps to ensure that new appetites, indulgences, and technologies do not compound our impacts on nature.

We have all observed some of these negative changes in our daily lives, yet we also know that many of the things that we care about can be maintained and sometimes restored. There is joy in watching the condor soar, the peregrine stoop, and the buffalo roam, and we experience an eerie joy in hearing the wolf howl—all have been brought back from the brink of extinction. The relevant questions may be both "What can be done to promote an era of sweeping change in attitudes and lifestyles," and "Who or what can do it?" Oddly enough, it is plausible that national parks can matter in unintended ways in any future scenario whereby humans must either throttle back on what we ask of the earth or find our way back—retracing our steps to a state of closer harmony with nature.

National parks could play an important role in laying out an unbiased, careful appraisal of environmental trends and trajectories—and spreading that knowledge from their platform of broad public access and respect. A technically stronger science effort might provide the roadmaps, the blueprints, and the genetic building materials for finding our way back from our collective trampling of the earth's biodiversity. These new roles are important reasons why parks matter, and it is in this urgent context that both the National Park System and the National Park Service must be reconsidered.

To be viable in an "archive of nature" role, a full representation of a nation's heritage must be protected. The current process for selecting national parks has, as we have seen, been haphazard and subject to political vagaries. There are always trade-offs when placing restraints on land use, and national park designation is no exception. For a small, vocal, and often locally effective segment of the American public, the national park idea is simply a tool for "big government" control. That fear is both real—parks often require restraints of traditional uses—and self-serving at the same time. But national parks create many other opportunities that make communities neighboring them the most prosperous and fastest growing in the nation. "Locking up the land," as in control of resource use, is also real in the same sense that a savings account or pension fund is a tyranny of financial restraint. Many communities understand that the rate of return from having national parks in their neighborhoods is significant and aggressively seek them; still others staunchly oppose them.

What may be unquantifiable in the calculation of the fairness of creating national parks in any local community or state is the element of serving the common public good. There is an element of national pride that ought to be valued—and tapped—in any local decision affecting the representation of the nation's natural heritage. Mike saw a glimpse of this when a midwestern family arrived in Washington with a large framed picture of their own prairie pothole—a small jewel of valuable waterfowl habitat on their land that they had asked be considered for designation as a National Natural Landmark. This family was proud of their land and their voluntary commitment to protect it. They came to Washington wanting to see their picture hung in the halls of the Interior building. That took some doing, but it may still be there to this day. And Mike still has the photo of their family posing on their land in front of their natural landmark plaque, with the American flag fluttering in the background—perhaps a noble environmental counterpart to Grant Wood's famous painting *American Gothic*.

A concerted effort to protect our national heritage can begin with national leaders who inspire national patriotism as well as local pride and sacrifice for the common good. Perhaps this can dampen the "not in my backyard" reaction that so often quickly scuttles a national park designation in the current political process. If one were to answer President Kennedy's call to "ask not what your country can do for you, but what you can do for your country," being involved in the creation (or protection) of a national park provides one of the best answers we know. It will take a willing public—indeed, a national movement—to assemble a science-based representative system of protected areas to serve us all in the present and in a potentially troubled future. A truly representative National Park System should be a transcendent priority for our nation.

The U.S. National Park System has been foremost in the world as a leader in developing the national park idea; it should remain so both in concept and in daily practice. To manage a national park system that will always matter requires an extraordinary intellectual effort and emotional attachment. Maintaining the ecosystem health of many millions of acres of complex ecosystems while providing visitor access may not be rocket science—it may be harder. Hence, as the world changes rapidly, both the system and the National Park Service must be consciously reconfigured to weather those changes. The price tag for this is not great in the overall federal outlay; it is largely a matter of awareness, prudent priorities, and will.

In few world arenas can so much be gained for so little as in protected-area establishment and prudent management. It is the intergenerational covenant for protecting a representation of the natural world we inherited that can lead the way in maintaining the natural diversity and health of the planet.

Modest changes in the current approach to building and managing the National Park System would do much to preserve national parks in the twenty-first century, but more than modest changes are needed if we are to effectively overcome the challenges confronting these unique landscapes and support the extraordinary roles they could play in tomorrow's landscape and in the psyche of the changing American public.

National parks can endure only if lifted above political skirmish and interagency rivalry. Our common national heritage is relevant to all citizens, and protection of that heritage should be part of the concern of all political parties and every state and federal agency. National parks must be removed from the daily battles and small visions that will lead to their death by a thousand cuts. National leaders must not tolerate petty turf battles at any level where the nation's natural heritage is at stake.

Each of our great national parks is irreplaceable. And, as a whole, America's National Park System, even as incomplete as it now stands, is a magnificent array that is a beacon to the world. We should try to imagine what Cape Cod, Yellowstone, Point Reyes (designated just ahead of twelve thousand planned condominiums), Great Smoky Mountains, or Redwood NPs would look like today if societal foresight had not provided the protection of national park status.

The National Park Service is a fine agency asked to do great and difficult things. It must be strengthened to a point at which it is up to the complex tasks necessary to keep its American covenant. We must avoid retooling the National Park Service without adding enhanced professionalism as its core. If it remains too tightly bound to the memories of its early success and its comfortable tradition of simple approaches to complex problems, the National Park Service will fail.

New leaders with new skills, backed by informed visitors, powerful partnerships, neighboring communities, and the public at large are the best combination for future success.

Protected systems that are maintained or restored to the highest level of ecological integrity and inherent resilience are invaluable assets. The specter of climate change highlights the value of our investment in national parks. Healthy systems will not be unaffected, but they will be the least affected and the most comfortable havens for the plants and animals that support us. Well-managed protected areas can be the navigational aids needed in a future in which environmental changes happen at an unprecedented rate.

There is little time to lose in developing a science-based understanding that includes ecological processes, strengths and vulnerabilities, and the kinds of steps necessary to minimize impacts both locally and globally. A place to begin is shoring up weaknesses in park science. Both internal NPS and external academic levels of participation in park science need overhauling. The education and communications efforts of national parks need a serious upgrade. Current assets that work must be protected and new levels of investment in science and science communication must be found.

But beyond a representational array of nature reflected in the units of the National Park System and the retooling of the National Park Service to meet modern challenges, new roles (laboratory, intellectual hub, trusted guide, and catalyst in tomorrow's changing landscape) can flow from a realistic interpretation of the mission statement in the Organic Act of 1916. Those roles can make the National Park Service singularly important in shaping our uncertain ecological future.

New roles are high hurdles. Given organizational inertia plus the often zigzag direction afforded by successive administrations, there is danger, and even a likelihood, that the National Park Service will repeatedly revert to its default mode—the strong focus on visitor services and park operations that was so successful until the late twentieth century.

The highest return from the National Park System will accrue if the staff of each park become trusted voices for environmental understanding, outreach, and ethic. As each park staff becomes authoritative on how their park's piece of nature works, how it has evolved, and where it is headed, that information can be transferred to the large portion of the American public who are curious and concerned. That fraction can make a huge difference in the decisions that shape the ecology and quality of life of our nation.

Many of us associated with the National Park Service realize that the awesomeness of the natural resources in national parks has by association made it appear an even better agency than it is. When the National Park Service is frequently voted the most popular government agency, the public is attesting to the powerful appeal of park resources and to the fact that in most cases their past management has not spoiled—and has often enhanced—their visit. The richness of experiencing our heritage has thus given the National Park Service great license with the public, license not only to develop visitor services and infrastructure but also to enhance the relationships between visitors and resources through new levels of engagement and information.

Perhaps despite the best efforts of the National Park Service, some parks may seem destined to fail. As we have seen, Everglades NP requires difficult and expensive effort if it is to regain the basic processes responsible for its original grandeur. Whether any forward-thinking agency could have stopped the centuries-old mania for wetland drainage in the subtropical paradise that is South Florida is doubtful. But early awareness, understanding, and a science-informed call for help might have better shaped the almost inevitable development that has so diminished this irreplaceable ecosystem.

The lesson is clear. Understanding, awareness, and communication are our best hopes for protecting natural systems to the maximum extent possible. We learned this too late in the Everglades, but the fact that precious remnants still evoke that earlier system is a basis for hope. The Everglades restoration saga attests that a thorough understanding of ecosystem vulnerabilities must precede any attempt to restore or "fix" them. "First do no harm" applies to park ecosystems as well as medicine.

In *The Prince* (1513), Niccolò Machiavelli wrote: "It happens then as it does to physicians in the treatment of consumption, which in the commencement is easy to cure and difficult to understand; but when it has neither been discovered in time nor treated upon a proper principle, it becomes easy to understand and difficult to cure. The same thing happens in state affairs; by foreseeing them at a distance, which is only done by men of talents, the evils which might arise from them are soon cured; but when, from want of foresight, they are suffered to increase to such a height that they are perceptible to everyone, there is no longer any remedy."[3]

Each park should provide a menu of options that encourage citizen science, engagement in science issues, and exploration of the trends that will affect the park's future as well as each citizen's own quality of life. Parks should be places that identify important environmental affairs and inspire further debate, and also speed the development of foresight on difficult issues such as climate change before there no longer is a realistic remedy. Thoreau said that our communities should be our universities. National parks can help with that.

The potential of national parks to serve broader roles needed by our society is unmatched. Parks—and, by extension, the National Park Service—begin with innate credibility provided by the authenticity of their resources. National parks provide unembellished windows into nature. Visits provide substantial opportunities for inspiring life-changing experiences and insight. National parks are places where messages must be unadulterated by political cant and fashionable trends. Objective science and its mode of discovery is a human offering that can significantly enhance the authentic experience of nature in national parks. Each park must become the focus for providing the experiences and awareness that will grow the community of support needed to meet future challenges head on. That constituency, by electing and working with an enlightened Congress, can elevate the role of national parks in shaping our environmental future.

It is challenging that at the time we were beginning to understand the meaning and implications of maintaining complex systems of nature unimpaired the task became yet more complicated. Perhaps the park protection quest can be the root of a larger understanding and accommodation by our species, starting with better sharing of experiences and responsibilities with the American population that visits parks.

Closing Thoughts

Our journey has taught us that the stakes for our national parks are much higher than most realize and that so much more should be expected from our National Park System. It has led us to believe that the golden age of national parks is yet to come. But it will not come if left to the old National Park Service. It will not come from Congress and the White House unless they hear the message of the covenant from the American public.

We have come to believe that within America's best idea, as expressed in the directive of the Organic Act, may be found the germ of an answer to a sustainable relationship with nature and the basis for a new environmental ethic. Rather than resting on early laurels, national parks can be sources of the knowledge, ideas, and vision that society sorely needs for shaping a better future. Within the physical reality of national parks rests the inspirational vitality necessary for these parks to continue to be associated with generating America's consequential ideas.

Rather than discount national parks as no longer pristine ("or natural") because of human footprints or human interference in global processes, we can alternatively see parks as dynamic and ever-fresh manifestations of nature. Rather than dismiss national parks as noble relics that must gradually succumb to universal declines in the quality of life on our planet, we can fiercely protect national parks as gold standards for environmental quality and national pride, in the best of times and in the worst.

Our present world is one of imbalance in key areas. Developed countries consume lavishly. Developing countries are causing severe impacts as they strive to reach the standard of living available in developed countries. Most countries also have large imbalances in wealth distribution, and there is no end to rampant consumerism in sight.

In the current world of wealth imbalance, those with substantial financial resources can look toward the national park idea and consider national parks as one of the finer legacies available in which to invest and to leave for future generations. Upon the achievement of wealth, what option to build a legacy can be more significant than contributing to the health and enjoyment of our country and our planet—and our fellow species? Certainly human health and well-being are popular causes for current-day philanthropy, but protecting the basic conditions that make the universal panoply of human experience possible would seem a fundamental investment of unparalleled lasting value.

There are magnificent examples of past and current philanthropic efforts, especially in America's past, and ongoing participation here and abroad. Yet there needs to be a new movement within philanthropic circles to bring a strategic application of resources that ensures

Death Valley National Park.
National parks connect and center us in the full scale of our existence. From
the immensity of the universe to the warmth of a campfire, national parks
matter for those connections. (Courtesy of the U.S. National Park Service)

that our American covenant is kept and widely shared. So much more can be done with what is already protected if there's a broader partnership of government, academe, private landowners, and those able to add to their legacy with service or gifts that contribute to the legacy of the American covenant. We all must do something at whatever level we can bear.

National parks matter because they are places that can center us in the universe. They connect us to the awesomeness of the night sky as well as the diversity of life about us. They remind us of where we began and how little we know about our beginnings. A park experience whispers to us that the human experience reaches far beyond the human species—that we are in fact a mere strand in the web of life.

Parks reconnect us to the full realm of life we no longer encounter in our daily lives and that we tend to forget—from majestic bison to tiny microbe or the lowly varmint that fascinated Henry's family in the Great Smokies. That is why parks matter.

National parks bond us to our land—the wondrous natural heritage of this great nation. Our personal reaction to parks demonstrates that we are indeed citizens of our physical place and its biological community with obligations far beyond our own identity as human. Parks remind us of the simple elegance and truth of nature, and experiences in parks can inspire us to seek a sustainable relationship between our daily lives and nature. That, too, is why parks matter.

Our American covenant to keep parks unimpaired is not only between our present society and future generations but also with the universal processes that brought us here. It is a covenant that honors and can prolong our stay and our joy as a contemplative species. Keeping our covenant demands we complete the National Park System, provide the research to understand park resources, restore their health whenever necessary, minimize unacceptable impacts whenever possible, teach an environmental ethic, show these things to our children, and maintain our vigil. In our time it will mean increased financial commitment, intellectual effort, and personal asceticism. Tactically it will require the application of place-based knowledge in restoring the health and natural resilience of every park, as well as greater educational outreach at home and abroad. These are within our reach. Parks matter, for their fate is our own.

Notes

Chapter 1. Good Fortune

1. M. S. Douglas, *Everglades: River of Grass* (Coconut Grove, Fla.: Hurricane House, 1947), 408.

2. Adapted from W. B. Robertson, Jr., *Everglades: The Park Story* (Homestead, Fla.: Florida National Parks and Monuments Association, 1989), 83.

3. Preserves are a special category that legislatively allows resource extractions or uses.

4. A frequently used estimate of the decline of wading birds in the Everglades is 90 percent, although there is great difficulty in interpreting historical records and trends. See G. T. Bancroft, "Status and Conservation of Wading Birds in the Everglades," *American Birds* 43 (1989): 1258–65; see also J. C. Ogden, "A Comparison of Wading Bird Nesting Colony Dynamics (1931–1946 and 1974–1989) as an Indication of Ecosystem Conditions in the Southern Everglades," as amended in *Everglades: The Ecosystem and Its Restoration,* ed. S. M. Davis and J. C. Ogden (Delray Beach, Fla.: St. Lucie Press, 1994), 533–70.

5. W. R. Burch, Jr., *Daydreams and Nightmares: A Sociological Essay on the American Environment* (New York: Harper and Row, 1971).

6. Buckingham Smith, "Report of Buckingham Smith," *Senate Document* 242, 30th Cong., 1st sess., August 12, 1848, 34.

Chapter 2. Our Sense of National Parks

1. J. R. McNeill, *Something New Under the Sun: An Environmental History of the Twentieth-Century World* (New York: W. W. Norton, 2000).

2. See, for example, E. Kolbert, *The Sixth Extinction: An Unnatural History* (New York: Henry Holt, 2014).

3. Pope Francis, *On Care for Our Common Home: Encyclical Letter Laudato Si' of the Holy Father Francis* (Vatican: Libreria Editrice Vaticana, 2015), 7.

4. Thich Nhat Hanh, *The World We Have: Approach to Peace and Ecology* (Berkeley, Calif.: Parallax, 2008), 1–2.

5. There is a long shelf of excellent histories of America's national parks. Many emphasize a particular perspective; some are scholarly, others of general interest. See for example: D. Duncan and K. Burns, *The National Parks: America's Best Idea* (New York: Knopf, 2011); W. C. Everhart, *The National Park Service* (Nashville: Routledge, 1982); R. A. Foresta, *America's National Parks and Their Keepers* (Washington, D.C.: RFF, 1984); A. Runte, *National Parks: The American Experience* (Boulder: Taylor Trade Publishing, 2010); D. E. Taylor, *The Rise of the American Conservation Movement: Power, Privilege, and Environmental Protection* (Durham: Duke University Press, 2016).

6. See, for example, M. D. Spence, *Dispossessing the Wilderness: Indian Removal and the Making of the National Parks* (New York: Oxford University Press, 1999), viii, 190; R. Keller and M. Turek, *American Indians and National Parks* (Tucson: University of Arizona Press, 1998), 319; and P. Burnham, *Indian County, God's Country: Native Americans and the National Parks* (Washington D.C.: Island, 2000).

7. M. D. Spence, "Dispossessing the Wilderness: Yosemite Indians and the National Park Ideal, 1864–1930," *Pacific Historical Review* 65, no. 1 (1996): 27–59.

8. National Park Service, "Frequently Asked Questions," https://www.nps.gov /aboutus/faqs.htm (last accessed September 21, 2018).

9. OXFAM International, "Richest 1 Percent Bagged 82 Percent of Wealth Created Last Year—Poorest Half of Humanity Got Nothing," last modified January 22, 2018, https://www.oxfam.org/en/pressroom/pressreleases/2018-01-22/richest-1-percent-bagged-82-percent-wealth-created-last-year (accessed September 21, 2018); L. Elliott, "Inequality Gap Widens as 42 People Hold Same Wealth as 3.7bn Poorest," *The Guardian Online* (January 21, 2018), accessed September 21, 2018, https://www.the guardian.com/inequality/2018/jan/22/inequality-gap-widens-as-42-people-hold-same-wealth-as-37bn-poorest.

Chapter 3. How National Parks Serve the Nation

1. The full quote attributed to Stegner is "National parks are the best idea we ever had. Absolutely American, absolutely democratic, they reflect us at our best rather than our worst." And many attribute the phrase "America's best idea" to Stegner, reinforced by Ken Burns's documentary series on the National Parks of America. Specific evidence that he wrote or uttered the quote, however, is lacking. Stegner himself deferred to James Bryce, an Englishman and ambassador to the United States, writing, "If the national park idea is, as Lord Bryce suggested, the best idea America ever had, wilderness preservation is the highest refinement of the idea." See A. J. MacEach-

ern, "Who Had 'America's Best Idea'?" *NiCHE* (October 2011), https://niche-canada
.org/2011/10/23/who-had-americas-best-idea.

2. R. W. Sellars, *Preserving Nature in the National Parks: A History,* 2nd ed. (New Haven: Yale University Press, 2009), 404.

3. A. Runte, *National Parks: The American Experience* (Lincoln: University of Nebraska Press, 1979).

4. H. Albright (as told to Robert Cahn), *The Birth of the National Park Service: The Founding Years, 1913–1933,* An Institute of the American West Book (Salt Lake City: Howe Brothers, 1985), 340.

5. D. Duncan and K. Burns, *The National Parks: America's Best Idea* (New York: Knopf, 2011), 22.

6. Ibid.

7. National Park Service, "Great Smoky Mountains National Park," https://www.nps.gov/grsm/learn/nature/index.htm (accessed March 2020).

8. U. S. Department of the Interior (Office of Congressional and Legislative Affairs), "Statement of Dale Ditmanson, Superintendent, Great Smoky Mountains National Park Before the Senate Subcommittee on National Parks, of the Committee on Energy and Natural Resources, concerning the All Taxa Biodiversity Inventory within the Great Smoky Mountains National Park," July 21, 2008, https://www.doi.gov/ocl/hearings/110/BiodiversityAtGreatSmokyMountains_072108; see the Discover Life in America website, https://www.dlia.org.

9. D. H. Janzen and W. Halwachs, "All Taxa Biodiversity Inventory (ATBI) of Terrestrial Systems: A Generic Protocol for Preparing Wildland Biodiversity for Non-damaging Use," in *Report of a National Science Foundation Workshop,* April 16–18, Philadelphia, Pa., 1993, 132.

10. H. D. Thoreau, *The Journal of Henry David Thoreau, 1837–1861,* ed. Damon Searls (New York: NYRB Classics, 2009), 704.

11. T. D. Brock, "The Value of Basic Research: Discovery of *Thermus aquaticus* and Other Extreme Thermophiles," *Genetics* 146, no. 4 (1997): 1207–10.

12. C. M. MacKenzi, G. Mittlelhauser, A. Miller-Rushing, R. B. Primack, "Floristic Change in New England and New York: Regional Patterns of Plant Species Loss and Decline," *Rhodora Journal* (January–March 2019). For examples of related management questions facing the managers of protected areas in today's landscape, see also R. Primack, A. Miller-Rushing, and R. T. Corlett, "Biodiversity Gains? The Debate on Changes in Local- vs. Global-Scale Species Richness," *Biological Conservation* 219 (2018): A2.

13. K. M. Newton, M. McKown, C. Wolf, H. Gellerman, T. Coonan, D. Richards, A. L. Harvey, N. Holmes, G. Howald, K. Faulkner, B. R. Tershy, and D. A. Croll,

"Response of Native Species 10 Years After Rat Eradication on Anacapa Island, California," *Journal of Fish and Wildlife Management* 7 (June 2016): 72–85; T. C. Boyle, *When the Killing's Done* (Chicago: Viking, 2011).

14. Unlike national parks, which are created by acts of Congress, national monuments are established by presidential proclamation under the Antiquities Act of 1906, which gives presidents the authority to declare and reserve "historic landmarks, historic and prehistoric structures, and other objects of historic or scientific interest that are situated upon the lands owned or controlled by the Government of the United States" (P.L. 59-209, Sec. 2).

15. National Park Service, "2018 National Park Visitor Spending Effects—Economic Contributions of National Park Visitor Spending," *Natural Resource Report* NPS/NRSS/EQD/NRR-2019/1922.

Chapter 4. National Park Realities and the Everglades Wake-Up Call

1. The following section is based on Mike's experience, files, and recollections of his time in the Everglades.

2. W. B. Robertson, Jr., *Everglades: The Park Story* (Homestead, Fla.: Florida National Parks and Monuments Association, 1989).

3. For a colorful treatment of Everglades history, including the water quality lawsuit, see M. Grunwald, *The Swamp: The Everglades, Florida, and the Politics of Paradise* (New York: Simon and Schuster Paperbacks, 2006), 458.

4. J. DeWitt, "Civic Environmentalism: Alternatives to Regulation in States and Communities," *Congressional Quarterly* (1994): 125–201.

5. M. E. Dorcas, J. D. Willson, R. N. Reed, R. W. Snow, M. R. Rochford, M. A. Miller, W. E. Meshaka, Jr., P. T. Andreadis, F. J. Mazzotti, C. M. Romagosa, and K. M. Hart, "Severe Mammal Declines Coincide with Proliferation of Invasive Burmese Pythons in Everglades National Park," *Proceedings of the National Academy of Sciences* 109, no. 7 (2012): 2418–22.

Chapter 5. National Parks as American Covenants

1. A. S. Leopold (chairman), S. A. Cain, C. M. Cottam, I. N. Gabrielson, and T. L. Kimball, *Wildlife Management in the National Parks,* transcript of the North American Wildlife and Natural Resources Conference (Washington, D.C.: Wildlife Management Institute, 1963), 32, 34, 43.

2. National Park Service (U.S. Department of the Interior), *Management Policies 2006,* Section 4.1 (Washington, D.C.: U. S. Government Printing Office, 2006), 168.

3. National Park System Advisory Board, *Revisiting Leopold: Resource Stewardship in the National Parks 2012*, www.nps.gov/calltoaction/pdf/leopoldreport_2012.pdf (accessed August 25, 2019), 11 .

4. See, for example P. Gonzales, F. Wang, M. Notaro, D. J. Vimont, and J. W. Williams, "Disproportionate Magnitude of Climate Change in United States National Parks," *Environmental Research Letters* 13 (2018): 104001, doi:10.1088/1748-9326/aade09.

5. National Parks Second Century Commission, "Advancing the National Park Idea," *Committee Reports* (Washington, D.C.: National Parks Conservation Association, 2009), www.npca.org/resources/1900-national-parks-second-century-commission-report.

6. National Park Service, *Management Policies 2006,* Section 4.1.

7. M. A. Soukup and J. W. Portnoy, "Impacts from Mosquito Control–Induced Sulphur Mobilization on a Cape Cod Estuary," *Environmental Conservation* 13, no.1 (1986): 47–50.

8. P. Kareiva and M. Marvier, "What Is Conservation Science?," *Bioscience* 62, no. 11 (2012): 962–69.

9. E. Duffin, "Number of Registered Active Lobbyists in the United States from 2000 to 2019," *Statista,* February 5, 2020, https://www.statista.com/statistics/257340/number-of-lobbyists-in-the-us.

10. G. E. Machlis and J. Jarvis, *The Future of Conservation in America: A Chart for Rough Water* (Chicago: University of Chicago Press, 2018).

Chapter 6. Navigating the Future

1. Theodore Roosevelt, "Doing as Our Forefathers Did," speech given on July 4, 1886, in Dickinson, Dakota Territory, Roosevelt Center at Dickinson State University, https://www.theodorerooseveltcenter.org (last accessed May 1, 2020).

2. World Bank Population Data Bank 2019, https://data.worldbank.org/indicator/sp.pop.totl.

3. J. R. MacNeill, *Something New Under the Sun: An Environmental History of the Twentieth-Century World* (New York: W. W. Norton, 2000).

4. See G. Scherer, "Christian-Right Views Are Swaying Politicians and Threatening the Environment," *Grist,* October 28, 2004, https://grist.org/politics/scherer-christian/; J. Hinderaker, " 'Rapture' Rapture," *Washington Examiner,* February 14, 2005, https://www.washingtonexaminer.com/weekly-standard/rapture-rapture. See also J. G. Watt, interview by Patty Limerick, Center of the American West, University of Colorado, Boulder, February 11, 2004, www.centerwest.org/wp-content/uploads/2011/01/watt1.pdf, 16.

5. D. Krahe, "The Ill-Fated NBS: A Historical Analysis of Bruce Babbitt's Vision to Overhaul Interior Science," in *Rethinking Protected Areas in a Changing World:*

Proceedings of the 2011 George Wright Society Conference on Parks, Protected Areas, and Cultural Sites (Hancock, Mich.: George Wright Society, 2012), 169–75. See also H. R. Pulliam, "The Political Education of a Biologist, Part I," *Wildlife Society Bulletin* 26, no. 2 (1998): 200–201; H. R. Pulliam, "The Political Education of a Biologist, Part II," *Wildlife Society Bulletin* 26, no. 3 (1998): 499–503.

6. Presidential Proclamation No. 2033, July 2, 1932 (47 stat. 2558), under provisions of the Antiquities Act of 1906.

7. United States District Court for the District of Colorado, 03-WY-1712.

8. Ibid.

9. "The Trump Administration Is Reversing 100 Environmental Rules. Here Is the Full List," *New York Times,* https://www.nytimes.com/interactive/2020/climate/trump-environment-rollbacks.html?action=click&module=Top%20Stories&pgtype=Homepage (accessed July 25, 2020), and G. Machlis and J. Jarvis, *The Future of Conservation in America: A Chart for Rough Water* (Chicago: University of Chicago Press, 2018).

10. K. Brower, "Leave Wilderness Alone," *Outside Online,* last modified October 13, 2014.

11. C. Rogers and J. Beets, "Degradation of Marine Ecosystems and Decline of Fishery Resources in Marine Protected Areas in the U. S. Virgin Islands," *Environmental Conservation* 28, no. 4 (2001): 312–22.

12. National Park Service, "Biscayne National Park Fishery Management Plan, Record of Decision 7-10-14," last modified November 2014, https://home.nps.gov/bisc/learn/management/upload/BISC-FMP-FEIS-APR-2014.pdf.

13. National Parks Second Century Commission, *Advancing the National Park Idea: National Parks Second Century Commission Report* (2009), www.npca.org/resources/1900-national-parks-second-century-commission-report.

14. R. F. Noss, D. S. Wilcove, J. Berger, and W. Karesh, "Letter to the Honorable Ken Salazar, Secretary of the Interior." Author Soukup received a personal copy on September 30, 2009.

15. Ibid.

16. NOAA, "Analysis of U.S. MPAs," *Marine Protected Areas Online,* https://marineprotectedareas.noaa.gov/dataanalysis/analysisus/ (last accessed April 7, 2019).

17. National Academy of Public Administration (NAPA), *Protecting Our National Marine Sanctuaries: A Report by the Center for the Economy and the Environment* (Washington, D.C.: NAPA, 2000), 118.

18. J. Miller, E. Muller, C. Rogers, R.W.A.A. Atkinson, K.R.T. Whelan, M. Patterson, and B. Witcher, "Coral Disease Following Massive Bleaching in 2005 Causes

60 Percent Decline in Coral Cover on Reefs in the US Virgin Islands," *Coral Reefs* 28, no. 925 (2009): https://doi.org/10.1007/s00338-009-0531-7.

19. J. Pelzer, " 'I'm Glad I Lost': Hansen at First Fought Grand Teton Expansion," *Casper Star Tribune,* October 22, 2009.

20. L. G. Brown, *Totch: A Life in the Everglades* (Gainesville: University Press of Florida, 1993), 269.

Chapter 7. Correcting Course

1. National Research Council, *A Report by the Advisory Committee to the National Park Service on Research* (Washington, D.C.: National Academies Press, 1963), https://doi.org/10.17226/21504, 156.

2. National Research Council, *Science and the National Parks: Committee on Improving the Science and Technology Programs of the National Park Service* (Washington, D.C.: National Academies Press, 1992), 122.

3. Ibid., 56–57.

4. R. Sellers, *Preserving Nature in the National Park* (New Haven: Yale University Press, 1997), 380; R. Sellers, *Preserving Nature in the National Parks: A History with a New Preface and Epilog,* 2nd ed. (New Haven: Yale University Press, 2009).

5. National Parks Second Century Commission, *Advancing the National Park Idea: National Parks Second Century Commission Report* (2009), www.npca.org /resources/1900-national-parks-second-century-commission-report.

6. L. Gould and D. Duncon-Hubbs, "Analysis of Assaults upon National Park Rangers, 1997–2003," 2004, last modified November 30, 2004, http://npshistory .com/publications/ranger/nau-131.pdf.

7. H. W. Meyer, *The Fossils of Florissant* (Washington, D.C.: Smithsonian Books, 2003), 258.

8. M. A. Boza, *Costa Rica: Parques Nacionales/National Parks* (Madrid: Incafo, 1996), 352.

Chapter 8. Why Parks Matter

1. P. M. Vitousek, H. A. Mooney, J. Lubchenko, and J. M. Melillo, "Human Domination of Earth's Ecosystems," *Science,* n.s. 277, no. 5325 (July 25, 1997), 494–99. See also S. Pimm, *The World According to Pimm* (New York: McGraw-Hill, 2001), 304.

2. J. R. McNeill, *Something New Under the Sun: An Environmental History of the Twentieth-Century World* (New York: W. W. Norton, 2000), 358.

3. N. Machiavelli, and H. C. Mansfield (trans.), *The Prince,* 2nd ed. (Chicago: University of Chicago Press, 1998), 124.

Index

Page numbers in italic type refer to illustrations